*The Promise That Changes Everything:
I Won't Interrupt You*

Nancy Kline is a bestselling author and Founding Director of Time To Think, a global leadership development and coaching company she established in 1997. Her ongoing research through work with colleagues, professionals, executives and teams around the world continues to build the body of thought known as 'The Thinking Environment'. Nancy is also Visiting Faculty at Henley Centre for Coaching, Henley Business School, UK.

Born and raised in New Mexico, Nancy is now also a UK citizen and lives in Oxfordshire with her English husband, Christopher Spence.

The Promise That Changes Everything: I Won't Interrupt You

NANCY KLINE

PENGUIN LIFE

AN IMPRINT OF

PENGUIN BOOKS

PENGUIN LIFE

UK | USA | Canada | Ireland | Australia
India | New Zealand | South Africa

Penguin Life is part of the Penguin Random House group of companies
whose addresses can be found at global.penguinrandomhouse.com.

First published 2020
001

Copyright © Nancy Kline, 2020

The moral right of the author has been asserted

Set in 12/14.75 pt Dante MT Std
Typeset by Jouve (UK), Milton Keynes
Printed and bound in Great Britain by Clays Ltd, Elcograf S.p.A.

A CIP catalogue record for this book is available from the British Library

ISBN: 978–0–241–42351–6

www.greenpenguin.co.uk

MIX
Paper from
responsible sources
FSC® C018179

Penguin Random House is committed to a
sustainable future for our business, our readers
and our planet. This book is made from Forest
Stewardship Council® certified paper.

For Christopher

who is in every word

Praeterita Honorem

Peter Kline

who said I should write,
and who saved my life
so that I could

Contents

Introduction

Sometimes you're just standing there. You have a thought. And your life changes forever. Maybe you have had one of those moments. It happened to me when I was thirty-seven.

I was co-founder of a Quaker school in Maryland. All of the faculty and students had gone for the day, and I was gazing out my office window, looking across the playing fields to the woods. I was thinking about what more I could do with the rest of my life to make a difference in the world.

Out of nowhere came this question:

What is the one thing which, if it were to change, could change everything else for the better?

And an answer:

The quality of people's independent thinking.

That may not sound exciting to you. But I was ecstatic.

It made sense. What we do follows what we think. So if our thinking is good, our decisions and actions will be, too. If our thinking is rubbish, well, welcome to the world.

So all we had to do, I reasoned, was improve our thinking, our *independent* thinking, and *voilà*, we could change everything.

The tricky part would be how to do it. I had a few ideas. Not many. But that was good enough for me. 'Start with something,' they say. Just start.

This book, another thirty-seven years later, is the fourth big pause to capture findings from observations my colleagues and I have made in that search for 'how':

We have some answers now. They are tentative, as all good answers should be. But they are thrilling. And simple. And so far astonishingly dependable.

Those answers are developments of ten *ways of being* with each other. I call them 'the ten components of a thinking environment'. We will explore them in depth in a little while because when we live them, as a system of being, we and the world around us do begin to change.

This 'thinking environment' starts and ends with the promise not to interrupt each other. It really does. I know that sounds too simple a thing to change a life, much less a world. But that simple promise is loaded. Like an atom. Take it apart and you see an unimaginable force, a force that generates the brilliance of life, in this case the brilliance of independent thinking.

Here we will explore how this promise does that, and why, and how it can become the centrepiece of our lives.

It seems that about every ten years my colleagues and I look up and realize that over that period we have learned so much more, so many new insights have surfaced, so many people's lives and organizations and relationships have grown in beautiful new directions because of these findings, and so much new research has substantiated and explained our own that a new book almost writes itself. This is the latest.

This book is both the science of the promise not to interrupt, and the music of it. It is both journey and scrutiny, reason and irrepressible stirrings.

It reflects the experience we all have every day. We interrupt. And we are interrupted. We may be inured to its ravaging because it is just the way life has become. But each time it happens, we wince. Often we rage. It registers.

The book builds on that common experience, sharing these past ten years of work with people, with their teams and their leaders, with families and schools, with law firms, scientists, engineers, the military, the police, academics, business schools, doctors and medical teams, politicians, therapists, business coaches and medi-ators. The results resound. Yours can, too. Living the promise is the proof of its efficacy.

To glimpse this living of the promise of no interruption, I think we have to understand the nature of three things: independent thinking, interruption and the promise itself. I have divided the book into those three points of focus. Each is both philosophical and practical. And each draws on those conditions for independent thinking, 'the ten components of a thinking environment'. These ten ways of being with each other profoundly affect the quality of our thinking. In brief, they are: attention, equality, ease, appreciation, feelings, encouragement, information, difference, incisive questions and place. We will explore them in depth in a little while.

The book does propose ways to 'live' these components, to *become* a thinking environment by making and keeping this prom-ise not to interrupt. It offers glimpses into a life as rich as this. More than anything else, this book is a saunter, a stretch, a suggestion. We humans, I find, learn the profound things best from experience, not from instruction. We learn from living the complexity of the context, not from lurching through a list.

And so this book is a conversation with you. I hope it will allow you to imagine what can change for you and your world because you and others around you make this promise and begin to think for yourselves with new quality and grace. I hope you will see as well that this most powerful promise of no interruption can affect even our current most vicious societal scourge – polarization. And I hope that exploration will lift your heart.

I invite you to join me, as if we were actually together, thinking for ourselves and delighting mutually in our freed minds.

If this is your first acquaintance with the 'thinking environment', welcome.

If this is one of many years of your engagement with it, I am honoured.

PART ONE

Understanding Independent Thinking

1. The Difference

I won't interrupt you.

I promise.

I won't interrupt your words – or your *thoughts*.

Imagine it.

Imagine the relief, the possibilities, the dignity.

You now have ground that is yours. Unassailably. This is for you. Time to think. To feel. To figure out what you really want to say. To say it, to consider it. To change it. To finish your sentences, to choose your own words. To become – because you can trust the promise – a bit bold, even eloquent. To become *you*.

And because you *know* I will not interrupt you, you will *want*, when you finish, to know what I think, too, even if we disagree deeply. You open your heart. And because you in turn promise not to interrupt me, I open mine.

We all long for this, the promise of no interruption, the promise of interest, the promise of attention while we think, the promise of this much respect for us all as human beings. We long for that gentle, rigorous expanse that produces felt thinking and thoughtful feeling. Every day, in *every* interaction, vital or trivial, we hope for the kind of presence that lets our brains and hearts find themselves.

We were born for this. In fact, says the science, we were born expecting it. Our brains needed it to keep forming when we were infants, almost marsupially.

They still do. To stay fully *Homo sapiens* our minds and hearts need this promise.

And yet?

It is nowhere. We look around. We can't find it. We see only interruption. Our colleagues interrupt. Our professionals interrupt. Our beloveds interrupt. Our friends interrupt. We interrupt.

Where in your circles can you point to a single person who you are certain will not interrupt or stop you when you speak? Who in your circles has ever made this promise to you? And kept it? And have you ever made that promise to anyone?

Most likely not. That is the shocking truth. The one thing we can absolutely depend on in life is that we *will be* interrupted when we start to think.

In fact, according to the Gottman Institute in Seattle, three years ago the average listening time of even *professional listeners* was twenty seconds. Now it is eleven. Eleven seconds! And those of us who are paid to listen – coaches, therapists, doctors, managers, leaders, teachers, pastors, advisers – have paid for endless instruction in how to listen. But the instruction is effectively in how to insert, how to tailgate, how to justify the populating of silence with our own view. It is listening that expects us to interrupt. Or so it seems. Certainly, observably, it does not require us to promise not to.

And so we interrupt. All of us. Paid and not. Partners and parents. Leaders and learners. Wage earners and shareholders. We move through our days and years interrupting others and failing to foil it when others interrupt us.

And that matters. Interruption diminishes us. It diminishes our thinking. In the face of it, our *own* thinking barely has a chance to form. That means that our decisions are weaker; our relationships are thinner. Interruption of thinking is so destructive, in fact, that what we have produced as a species, however advanced it may be in the animal kingdom, is probably inferior to the achievements the uninterrupted human mind might have produced over those aeons instead.

In fact, you could mention just about any stubborn issue in your life and I would wonder whether you might have resolved it already had you not been interrupted so many times on the road to now. I also could name almost any innovation, from howling steam engines to hallowed cyberspace, and argue that humanity might well have thought of things more elegant and nourishing if our thinking had not been interrupted so much along the way.

Most vital questions human beings have asked through the ages – how can we educate? how can we heal? how can we earn? how can we govern? how can we judge? who should be rich and who poor? what is a nation and who are we anyway? who is right? – might have produced more sustainable, egalitarian, integrated, dignifying answers if we had not interrupted each other so often in conversations and meetings and musings, and if we also had not interrupted *ourselves* because others' interruptions over the years had convinced us we didn't have much to offer anyway.

And our relationships? I surely don't need to articulate the difference the promise of no interruption might have made in every single relationship since humans developed language. Think about yours. Imagine your relationships without interruption. Imagine the sweet, stimulating sturdiness that would grow from that promise. I often wonder if divorce figures would reduce dramatically if there had been a vow of no interruption at the wedding.

Then, as if interruption by each other were not enough to minister to the diminishment of our independent minds and the shrinking of meaning in our relationships, enter smartphones. More accurately 'hurtphones' or 'stupidphones'. With their built-in servicing of platforms that colonize our attention, they slap our brains into brainlessness. Relentlessly distracted, our thinking begins to haemorrhage.

This loss is not wholly the device's fault, of course. It is mostly ours. Even with the smartphones' on-purpose designed-in distraction notification architecture, our prostration at their non-human feet is the real issue. Our obeisance demotes the advanced human, and we pretend it doesn't. We don't take charge of our attention. Our little robots do. And we caress them.

This we can stop. We can stop all forms of interruption. (There are more than you think, and we will explore them all.) We can decide right now to be masters of our attention, to commit to the flourishing of our minds, of our hearts, of our very nature.

This attention, this promise not to interrupt, this act of breathing free, is prodigious. It changes things. Even the big things. It bestows sanity. It shapes and reveals and shapes again who we are.

e in the face of uncertainty. It can stop things like hatred
ings like love. It rescues our meetings from vacuity, cre-
us places to work, brings humanity to leadership and
to humanity. Attention, some have told me, is what we
god'.

It launches dreams. The dreams we have for ourselves, yes; but
also the dreams for our world. We all have them. Even the most
cynical of us. We've just grown wary and weary and willing to
walk away from each other, and from ourselves.

This promise of no interruption, this sustaining of generative
attention, can turn us towards each other.

In fact, the decision not to interrupt each other is powerful enough
to mitigate the prepotent relationship issue of our time, the issue
that cleaves our conversations at work, in politics, in religion,
between neighbours, in families and invisibly inside ourselves – the
societal bifurcation we call polarization. This contemporary scourge
is ancestral. And it is high time we faced it down by facing its cause.

*Polarization is not a result of disagreement. It is a result of disconnec-
tion.* When we disconnect from each other, when we see each other
no longer as human beings but as threats, we polarize. And the
first, most forceful disconnector is interruption.

I think that polarization in each instance, therefore, *starts* with, and
is fed by, interruption. The very first minute one of us in stark disagreement interrupts the other, the brain registers the interruption as
a *physical* assault. Immediately the brain hormones of adrenaline and
cortisol bathe the cortex, the very centre of our thinking; the amygdala, dictator of feelings, instantly dispatches the triumvirate actions
of freezing, fleeing, fighting. And presto, we disconnect. Our thinking shrivels. And polarization is born.

But I have seen people stop that cycle. I have seen them gather
instead, determined to understand each other, not to convince each
other. Crucially, they have arrived having promised to stop interrupting. They have agreed 1) to *start giving attention*, 2) to *stay
interested* in where each other's thinking will go next and 3) to 'share
the stage' equally.

The promise of no interruption consisting of those three ingredients changed their conversation forever. Polarization fizzled. New possibilities emerged. Those three ingredients walked forward together. Not into a sunset. It was better than that. They walked into the grit and gossamer of new thinking that springs from emotional integrity, understanding and mutual cherishing of the effects of this powerful promise.

I will not interrupt you.

It changes everything.

Good, you may be thinking. I'm in. But surely I don't need to read on? Can't I just take your point, go home, stop interrupting and, *tra-la*, change the world?

In theory, yes.

It *should* be enough for each of us just to notice this out-of-control, societally rewarded, devastating practice of interrupting, this wholesale, sanctioned violence against human independent thinking, and resolve to stop it today.

But it isn't. This practice of interrupting people's speaking and thinking is fed at an ideological level inside us. We think it is the right thing to do. We really do. Oh, we know it is not really polite or considerate, so sometimes we apologize as we do it. But we keep going. We think it is nearly always justified, and maybe even the very best thing that can happen at that moment. We think we are even saving time by knocking down the person talking while we hold forth.

Delusion takes some doing to undo.

First, we need really to *get* that interrupting is a violent act. To begin with, we need to understand what interruption *is*. We have to recognize all of its pernicious and artful forms.

And then we have to examine it at a 'cellular' level. We have to see the untrue assumptions that drive it, take them apart and start over with true ones.

Keeping the promise of no interruption is a tough job.

Tough because this promise is an unspiralling galaxy of a thing.

It stretches past our all-at-once field. It defies our gulping. Its whole cannot be parsed, and yet it has to be to be understood.

Every day over the years I have thought repeatedly that I had seen this promise in all its glory. I have thought each time I saw it that I had it down, that there was no more to see, no more to add to its definition or its effect. I have felt confident that I was doing it just as I wrote, as I taught, as I spoke, as I tried every day to live it. I have committed to its treasure and been sure I held it all in my arms. But before I could breathe out, I have, startled, seen it as if for the first time. And I have had to smile.

I also have seen people claim this promise, clip it to their listening portfolios, sell it as their skill set, and not come close. It is as if we can never know it. It is as if it is here and not here, evident and elusive, finished and foetal all at once.

I think this is because this promise is different from anything else we do with each other. I want to say that again. *This is different.*

It is different because it requires a donning of humility, a rich regard for difference and for 'other'. It is different because it upends the appearance of stability. It is different because it wants to, and does, produce *independent* thinking. And so it is subversive. Succouringly so. It is different because it requires us to stop wanting to impress and to start wanting to free. It changes what we call expertise. It changes what we charge for and pay for and what we reward. It can change our very purpose.

This promise and its luminous effects *are* different. But humans cannot see difference all at once. Our predispositions, our rituals, our norms – in this case interruption and its frayed and fractious outcomes – are our habituated context. They are our reference points for what is. So they are all we see.

We, therefore, have to fell those remorseless norms one by one in order to notice their radiant absence.

This felling begins by facing the emptiness of our excuses for interruption: 'I must clarify; I must correct; I must look smart right now; I must enrich; I must follow my *own* curiosity; I know where you are going with this; I need to take you elsewhere; your unformed thought will be less valuable than my formed one; I am more important than you are; I look stupid not talking; no one needs to listen this long; you will never stop.'

None of these is worthy of us.

So I hope that you will step away from that crepuscular culture and follow the first light: the soon-to-be-obvious power of this promise and of its effect on the intelligence in front of us. Including your own.

To stop interrupting –

1) to start giving attention
2) to sustain interest in where the person will go *next*
3) to 'share the stage' –

comprises possibly the simplest cluster of complex change we will ever make.

2. The Search

This all started with surrender. One day, just like that, I gave up. After three years of trying everything, I admitted I knew nothing. I was forty.

Three years before, I had set out to uncover the secrets of independent thinking. Armed with the insight that the quality of everything human beings do depends on the quality of the independent thinking we do first, I reasoned that to create the world we wanted, we had to think *for ourselves* well. And as far as I could see, hardly anyone was doing that.

I had thought listening would help. I had been among Quaker educators and among peer counsellors, so I tried all kinds of listening. Thirteen to be exact. I listened to understand, to reframe, to release feelings, to plan, to unblock, to challenge, to comfort, to solve, to interpret, to inform, to diffuse, to guide and to teach.

They were useful. But they didn't produce *independent* thinking. They helped with other things. And they produced good ideas sometimes. But no matter what kind of listening I did, people were not dependably thinking *for themselves*. Most of the time I was thinking for them. They probably wouldn't have put it that way. They were usually pleased with the outcomes. But I knew that my listening had taken them, however cunningly, to *my* idea of where they should go. And they had come along willingly.

I did not know how to keep their own thinking going. The weird thing was how fine they were with that.

I was not fine with it. It seemed to me that the world, and every individual life in it, needed *fresh* thinking, not guided, moulded, rewarded, derivative, compliant, samey thinking.

So one day I decided to throw out everything I knew and start from scratch. I couldn't really do that, of course, because who we are is where we have been. But I did my best. I walked away from the theories, processes and knowledge I had acquired through my study of various psychological and philosophical takes on the human psyche, and began again. What, I asked myself, was the very minimum I could do to ignite, but not influence, a person's own thinking? And what could I do to keep it going?

Eventually, I faced it. It was embarrassingly simple: be present and don't speak. (Later, of course, this simple notion turned out to be heaving with complexity.)

So, at-wits'-end intrepid, I decided to do that. To promise it, and to do it.

And *that* is what worked: I *promised*.

I asked people if they would be willing for me to try it with them. They were.

And it was astonishing. The thinking that emerged was every bit as good as, often better than, the thinking that had come from my oh-so-smart, guiding questions. *How could that be?* I agonized. I had not done anything. I had just sat there, saying nothing. And they knew I would. How could that be so effective? I was sleep-deprivingly curious about that. But I became afraid to wonder too hard about it for fear it would jinx everything. So I just kept doing it. I threw in this and that now and then, but the additions seemed to distract. Finally, I returned to those two simple things: be present and don't speak. I promised. And I kept the promise.

Along the way when they said they were truly finished, I was tempted to come in with something wise and wonderful from my vast and, of course, impressive knowledge and experience, with some drop-dead brilliant question that would leave them dazzled at, yes, me. But I gritted my teeth and plugged back into wondering whether they could think even further than that, *for themselves*.

Getting their own thinking to continue was a bit stumbley at first. Follow-ups like, 'Is that it?' or 'Are you finished?' or 'Keep going' didn't always do much. And certainly any question referencing *my* choice of their content flopped utterly. 'Can you tell me more about . . .?', 'I hear you saying that . . .', 'Have you thought about . . .?' and 'Could you imagine instead . . .?' were disasters. People went visibly from energized to enervated, from autonomous to anonymous, in a heartbeat.

So I stopped that and tried to find a 'say more' version of 'be present and don't speak'. After several years of stabbings in the dark I tried: 'What more do you think, or feel, or want to say?' It worked. They kept going, and I kept out of it.

I had feared they would think I had not been listening at all given that they had just said they were truly finished. But I was finding that where there has been some thinking, there can be more, given just the right encouragement. And almost always, which if you think about it is amazing, the additional thinking they generated was usually even more valuable than their previous thoughts.

So I tried it again. And again. That same 'What more do you think, or feel, or want to say?' Until they really, really were finished, as in they had no response at all.

This became the whole focus of my work for a while. I was on a mission. At first I was doing all of it pro bono. Who was going to pay for me to say 'nothing'?

But so many people said it was the most valuable listened-to experience they had ever had. Really? So eventually I began to charge, and held my breath. They paid and did not hold theirs. They thanked me.

That bewildered me. What were they paying for? My presence and my silence and the same keep-going question asked over and over until it didn't work any more? Apparently. There was nothing else to pay for. Why, then, I had to ask myself again, was it producing such valuable results?

That question took a third of my life to answer. (In fact, my colleagues and I are still working on it; these answers are ever-emergent, it seems.)

During that time we discovered that inside this promise not to speak, this simple three-faceted agreement to stop interrupting (to start giving attention, to stay interested and to 'share the stage'), there is a lot going on. Inside this promise there appears to be a kind of 'coding' for removing blocks in thinking. It appears that the mind, when not interfered with, asks itself a range of catalytic, almost 'innate' questions when it gets stuck, breaking through blocks for itself, so it can be on its way again. All of that seems to happen when the promise of no interruption is in place and the mind is soaring.

And in that promise, too, there is a rich colony of catalysts. There are at least ten conditions – the 'components of a thinking environment' I mentioned, conditions we are providing when we give attention and don't speak. These 'components'– attention, equality, ease, appreciation, feelings, encouragement, information, difference, incisive questions and place – we will explore in fresh detail later. The point here is that they actually *generate* thought. To decide to live them is to decide to cherish independent human thinking.

So I think of this promise not to interrupt as a kind of zygote. Zygotes mesmerize me: one cell combines with another cell to become *one* cell. I adore that bit of mathematical defiance. And inside that new cell is the stuff of trillions of other cells and their heroic and resplendent expressions that collaborate to become an entirely unlikely entity of ineffable majesty: us.

I think that attention and interest are like that. Let them meet, and you create independent thinking – the singular, triumphant articulation of this wonder that is *Homo sapiens*. Could it be that attention and interest *create* thought, a 'being' that is loaded with the fire of life? I think so.

The ignition of independent thinking happens inside us when we experience attention and *know* we will not be interrupted. It is the *knowing*, the promise, that produces the trust that produces the courage that produces our new thinking.

So, most of the time, generative attention was enough. And it was splendid.

But sometimes it wasn't enough. Sometimes the person suddenly could not break through for themselves. They got stumped. They stopped. And I did not know what to do. I could not figure out how to help someone past a block while not steering them *at all*. I faked it for a while and we limped along. Eventually, probably desperate to extricate themselves from my sudden, uncharacteristic 'follow-me' utterances, they started thinking again and managed to break through for themselves.

Over time I pondered that: they *would* break through for themselves if they possibly could. I had 'seen' those moments. Over time I did my best to deconstruct their breakthroughs and to discern what they had just done for themselves.

Finally, I could see it. They had asked themselves a spectacular breakthrough question. And they had gotten there by asking themselves a cluster of other questions first. It was a logical and beautiful sequence, supple and able to leap from one snare to a question to a different snare to another question until it arrived finally at that most liberating question of all. In later years I would label that one an 'incisive question', because it was, indeed.

How fabulous, I realized. Maybe I could ask people those questions, ending in the incisive one, when they said they were stuck, instead of making them live through my lurches and collapses. I tried. It worked. Virtually every time.

And it still does. That cluster of questions (some of the 'innate' ones I mentioned) seems to be the mind's own life force.

I have said that we have also very recently begun to understand that the mind seems to think in 'waves and pauses', not in 'parts'. (Formerly I thought the road to the incisive question consisted of 'parts' and could be mapped. I was wrong. The mind is not so predictably linear.) It then determines in the pause the 'just right' question among those 'innate questions' to generate a new wave. As the listener, we are now able to navigate that same 'pause' process to determine the right question when the person cannot do it for themselves.

And so the journey continues. From the frustration, to the white flag, to the stripping down, to the trying, to the wondering, to the noticing, to the piecing together, to the being wrong, to the trying again, to the noticing again and the being wrong again, and the not turning away, to the impressive results and changed lives and organizations, and to the ongoing intrigue of the never-completely-there seeing of what works, of facing what doesn't and of watching the pursuit find itself.

Along the way we have created beautiful courses and qualifications and other elegant executions of what we are learning about

18

this way of being with people, this 'thinking environment'. But the abiding joy is in seeing that these ten conditions, these 'components', that populate the promise not to interrupt appear to work regardless of culture or background, status or personality type, religion or income, or even predisposition to being nice. Something innate does seem to be going on when we honour each other in this way. Something worth learning.

Something even worth living.

3. For Themselves

Do you want people to think well?

Yes. Most likely. At least I hope so.

But the real question is: do you want people to think *for themselves*?

I still hope so. But I'm dubious. Because that is different. Thinking *for ourselves* is different. Entirely.

And that difference is the absolute marrow, the quark 'inside' the proton, the point of the point of the point of this book. *Thinking for yourself is different.*

The difference between thinking and thinking for yourself changes not just the game, but the life. And *helping each other* to think for ourselves is so different it stops us in almost every track of helping we have ever mastered.

Thinking for ourselves is different from thinking. It is different from thinking well. It is different from solving, from understanding, from sorting, from factoring in, from seeing the path, from listing the pros and cons, from deciding, from noticing patterns, from seeing the blind spots, from establishing accountability, from being quiet, from telling the story and from doing cartwheels because, yippee, the equation finally works. Those are all fantastic. I wish them on everyone I know and love.

But that is not this. If what you want to do is to think *for yourself* as far as you possibly can before you need my thinking – that is *different*. Wonderfully, it will include all of those things, I promise you. But it will go way beyond them.

And here's the thing: that difference occupies nearly a world of its own. It reaches in and pulls out the most amazing aspects of ourselves. It finds pristine honesty and dazzles us. It employs courage we had no idea lived there. It gestates what we call creativity but can barely imagine. And it can challenge everything we thought we knew.

It's its own work of art. And we cannot, we simply cannot, know ahead of time how it is going to look at the end. We cannot plan it, shape it, do pre-work for it, pray for it, send for prototypes of it or hold it right there. Nothing we have done has prepared us for this. Not our life experience, and certainly not our professional qualifications. Nor our lore, nor our rituals, nor our lined-up, ready-to-go portfolios of how to be an if-only-I-could prize-winner of a helping person.

Drop those how-to-help things. They do not work. Not for generating a person's *own* thinking. Be present. That is what it takes. Be so present that the mind in front of you works differently.

For itself.

That's why I doubt it. I don't want to doubt it. I want to be confident as anything that you, that we all, want to do this, to think for ourselves and to help each other to do that – whatever it takes. However much peeling off we have to do of our tried and tired ways, however exposed we have to be in the night guard's torch of 'how it's supposed to be done', we *will* have to choose this difference. And maybe you are not that interested. Maybe you have come this far and want the perks of persistence that perpetuate the past. I understand that. Go well.

But if you are even a bit keen to see what might happen, what gems might emerge, what at first delicate but soon substantial changes might enlighten and then light up our world if only we could think for ourselves? Then you'll enjoy this.

4. The Decision

So, if independent thinking matters so acutely, how do we start?
We decide.
That's it.
We decide to produce independent thinking. In this moment, we *decide*. Action follows. But first we decide.
This moment is upending.
As 'thinker' we *decide* to care more about where our *own* thinking will go than we do about what people will think of it, or of us. As 'listener', we *decide* to care more about where the thinker will go next with *their* thinking than we do about imposing ours.
And then we stare down the temptation to destroy independent thinking as it emerges.
This *decision* to produce independent thinking is really, really, really different.
And until we get this difference, as in let it whoosh through our veins and gambol in our brains, reshaping the norm and forming a new priority, we will not really do it. We will falter. We will hover. We will stalk the peace of the thinker until they tense and give up. We will start wiggling our feet and then our legs and then we will raise our arms and clasp our hands behind our head and exhale. Then we will interrupt. We will destroy their autonomy in favour of our rule. This difference between derivative thinking (as in, derived from other people) and independent thinking is usually so unsettling we back off from deciding to choose it.
Perhaps that is because Martha Graham, the great choreographer, was right: 'Every decision is a sacrifice'. This is true both of what 'position' we take with our bodies as we dance and of what direction we take with our minds as we think.
And when we decide to generate independent thinking, we are sacrificing all the familiar wraiths of life like acquiescence,

belonging, norm-addiction and status. So the decision, this entirely different decision, is an act of courage.

Imagine this moment: You are talking. You are thinking. I am listening. You are alive. You step into that world of fully independent thinking. I keep listening. You keep thinking. Then. Without warning, I feel a need to speak. I nearly do. But having promised not to, I try to notice what is happening. I see, reluctantly, that I don't *have* to speak. I have choice.

So I decide at least to weigh up the risks. I remember writer Nassim Taleb's way of assessing financial risk (from his majestic book, *Antifragile*). I ask myself this question:

If I speak now, can I be sure that the upside from the gain of my already thought thoughts will be greater than the downside from the loss of your as yet unthought thoughts?

No, I admit, I cannot possibly be sure of that because neither of us knows what you have not yet thought. On the other hand, I do know what *I* have thought. So those thoughts are retrievable if needed later. I can just set them into my pretty come-back-later box here next to my antsiness.

But what you have not yet thought can be obliterated forever if I dive in before you have finished. And that loss of your thinking may be far greater than any gain from mine. I just don't know. And because *I don't know*, I do not make the sacrifice.

Or for brevity I might have formed the question in my mind this way:

Can I be sure that what I as the listener am about to say will be of more value than what you are about to think?

Of course not. For the same reasons. I have *no idea* what you are about to think. I think I do. I think I've 'got it'. I think I have heard enough of what you think to be sure I know what you are going to think next. But I don't. I absolutely don't.

How could I? For one thing, according to Ken Sergi, Organization

Development specialist, we think seven times faster than we speak. We speak at approximately 115 words per minute, but think at approximately 825 words per minute. My own experience aligns better with an even starker view offered by a psychologist on one of my courses. His working hypothesis is that 'for every thirty words we say, we don't say 300'. If he is right, even when I am listening to you beautifully, I don't have access to 90 per cent of your thinking. So surely we both benefit if you can develop your thinking fully before I speak. At least the 10 per cent I am responding to will be more accurate and fully formed, so my response can be, too.

A more important point, though, is that if the conditions are right, i.e. if I keep listening with deep interest in where you will go next, you will go next to places I could never have taken you. Places with far more magic and meaning and relevance.

So I do make a choice, but it is different. It is the choice that sacrifices the known for the unknown. I stay attentive, rapt. Generatively and generously.

I overcome the urge to speak.

You continue. Intact.

I want to say again that this decision to produce *independent* thinking is different from any other we make as listeners, as colleagues, as friends, parents, teachers. It is. And that overriding, glistening difference is so huge it is like a billion pirouetting photons headed our way.

There is also a rending insight about this difference. I heard it from one of my students, a business executive:

'Wanting people to do their own thinking, listening to ignite their as-yet unthought thoughts, as you say, is going to be, for me at least, a step-by-step journey towards humility.'

Yes. It is. That is exactly what it is. As listeners we decide to shine by not shining. And of all the differences between exchange thinking and *independent* thinking, between interruptive listening and generative attention, the 'journey towards humility' is surely the most uprooting.

But it is only the first journey. A needed one, an elegant one. But only the first.

The final journey is, ironically, the *end* of humility, because when we want independent thinking more than anything – when we cannot stand *not* to know what will evolve next in the mind of the thinker – humility is no longer the challenge. It has become the norm.

And when it is, when we know because we have seen it hundreds of times, that we *can* think brilliantly for ourselves, and that we *will* if the people with us keep the promise not to interrupt and to stay interested in where we will go next? And when they want us, fiercely, to keep thinking?

What then?

It *will* happen.

We *will* think for ourselves all the way to a place of quality and value neither of us could have divined.

This *decision* to produce independent thinking in ourselves and in others is monumental. It is an earthquake's earthquake. It is a way to meaning. It is a way to understanding. It is a way to the lives we long for. It is a way to the world most of us want, but speak of only in our personal silence.

We ache for it, this act of simplicity that teems with complexity, and smiles in our direction.

See? There it is.

We need only walk over and say hello.

Then why do we resist?

If thinking for ourselves is so great, so much fun, so full of self-discovery and meaning and sheer amazement, not to mention loaded with propitious implications for our world, why do we resist the decision to do it? Why as thinkers do we defer to others' thinking, and expect others as thinkers to defer to ours? Why is it that just about the only time we think for ourselves is when we are thinking for someone else?

Because when we were young, no one asked us this life-shaping question: 'What do *you* think?' And then listened because they wanted to know. No one. Most people grow up without that question. And without that attention. And what people don't experience in childhood, they don't expect in adulthood.

What a world this is. A child is born. It has equipment in its head (with sentries scattered elsewhere) so dazzling even Da Vinci would fail to render it. All it needs right now to work well and to keep unfolding is a particular kind of sustained attention, *generative* attention. And in a very short time it needs also that question, and more of the same attention. Yes, it needs information from sources as accurate and varied as possible. But attention and the question 'What do *you* think?' are the key means to their brain's lifelong purring.

But where is it, this attention? And where is it, this question? Nowhere.

Actually, sometimes the first few minutes of life are pretty good. Usually the newborn is placed in its mother's arms and into her intelligent, loving gaze. Again, that attention is generative because it continues the cellular development of the newborn's brain.

But very soon 'I'm listening' is nowhere to be found. 'What do you think?' Nowhere. 'Keep going, I'm interested.' Nowhere. 'Your mind is a treasure.' Nowhere.

So. Good thinking? Independent thinking? Not much of a chance. Not at the moment. But change is afoot. And the human mind will not be in this sutured state forever. In Part Three we will explore how different a human life might look if its inborn thinking capacities were not beleaguered from birth, if instead the 'nowhere things' were 'everywhere things'. It is beautiful.

And it is excruciatingly possible.

This deciding – what must we face to do it?

That we have a self.

That's a tough job in the grip of our be-like-me, do-it-only-this-way reward cultures. A big job. Too big for us most of the time, it seems.

We won't risk it. We won't risk overturning our allegiance to the forces that formed us. We won't risk even imagining that we might have a good brain; that we might be able to think as well as, even better than, the brains that birthed us and the ones that lead us, the ones who pay us, who stick that medal on our lives and shake our hand. To risk all that we must face that the persuaders we long to love are wrong.

And facing the wrongness of the master is a wrench. *Feeling*, rather than suppressing, our disappointment at allegiance stings. At first. But once we've done it, it is freedom unlike any other.

The self?

Yes. We do have a self, an intact, luminous core of intelligence. A core that deserves a fifty-times-a-day opportunity to express itself. We just have to decide. We can free that self from the made-up infrastructures of command that glare when that self peeks through. Glare back. Crawl out. Stand, lift your ribs, take in the sky. Decide.

I've witnessed this deciding, this resurrection of self, this cradling of core, thousands of times. Each time is a fresh revelation, a privilege.

What do you think? I want to know. I won't interrupt.

There is something about that question and those conditions that rescue the core self. Genuine is what the *core* self is. And it will emerge when genuine is what surrounds it.

What do you think?

I won't interrupt.

The self *will* arrive, if the road is right.

5. Two Things

This is what I think it takes.

Two things.

One, we have to get it, *really* get it, that one person's generative attention *produces* another person's new thinking.

Don't rush that.

Two, a person's generative attention loses its power the very second it wavers. Attention like this has to be *continuous*.

Take that in, too. It defies 3,000 years of instruction in how to listen.

This 'wavering' point is rooted in the fact that we can't *sort of* do this independent thinking thing. We either do it or we don't. We either want to think for ourselves or we don't. We either want other people to think for themselves, too, or we don't. We can mix a lot of things in life. But not this.

The pay-off, the truly oh-wow-I-never-thought-of-that-until-this-very-moment moment, waits until it absolutely knows it can trust the person's attention; it can trust that it will go on unfatigued, unseduced by the draw of mattering by talking. *Oh*, you may think, *I'll just grab this tiny pause here to say a little something.*

Forget it. You will kill all that was about to form. You might as well not have started.

In fact, we have to start noticing and admitting what is happening when we speak before the person invites us to. We have to notice that we have screeched them to a halt. We have erected a huge billboard with our picture on it right in their face and said: *Stop! Look at me. I know better than you what you need now. You need me to speak. I don't care where you would have gone in your thinking just then. I do not care. I care that you know what I think of what you were thinking (or more accurately what you were saying, because I have no idea at all what you were thinking that you did not say), but I don't care because*

I have lots to say about what you did say. And I care that you recognize my value to you because of what I am saying right now. Nope, I'm not through yet. You will be grateful to me for this. Oh, is your thread slipping away? Well, no problem. You have my thread now. Lucky you.

And it doesn't take much change in the listening quality for the thinker's mind to authorize advanced reconnaissance. It can detect imminent incursion before even LIGO could pick it up.

Yes, those two things:

Attention from one person produces fresh thinking in another.

Attention like that is seamless.

Once we know them, life is never the same again. It is better forever.

6. Trust the Thinker

Remember, too, that we can't know right this second what we don't know right this second. We can only stride out and trust. Also, we can't know that trusting will be worth the risk of abandoning what we know for something we don't.

That is a lot of not knowing. And humans are not brilliant at not knowing. We like to think we know everything. Even some very, very, very smart people have said things like, 'It seems probable that most of the grand underlying principles of life have been firmly established' (Albert Michelson, 1894), and 'The era of fundamental revelations in nature is over' (John Horgan, 2014).

Disquieting, I agree. But you need only look around yourself to see how your life defaults to knowing-for-sure. It would take you quite a few hours to count the things you do because you have already done them and you trust they work. But in only a few seconds you could count the things you did today that were conscious opposites of those trusted things. Two, three?

I counted three this week. I usually sleep eight hours. But on this morning I heard the blackbirds in the dawn chorus, swooned and decided to get up, go up to my study and just sit, listening.

And yesterday I wrote for two blissful hours before I did a single email.

And today I decided not to be the 'glue' of conversation when my six students were gathering over espresso. I moved to the circle of chairs where we would be learning in a few minutes and just sat, admiring them all.

In all of these moments there was that faint frisson in that split second when I turned my back on the usual and committed to the different.

That's all it is. Just a little zing. An 'if' feeling. A 'this might not work but no one will die' feeling. It's not a 'jeepers what have I done and who will I *be* after this?' feeling. To let go, even for a minute, of the thing that is familiar for the thing that is really not is only to shift from *ah* to *hmmm*. And that is actually kind of nice. And the good thing is Plan B. We can always go back to the familiar. It is there, arms crossed.

So it's not such a big deal to decide, for example, not to interrupt anyone or, before they are finished, not to interject your thoughts, for the next hour. What could go wrong? Just about the worst thing that could happen would be that they look at you strangely because they have memorized your interrupting pattern and you have suddenly become weirdly out of sync with yourself. But so what?

You could let them know ahead of time that you think that if you don't stop them, they will produce thinking they couldn't otherwise. You could do this not in order to save the familiar brilliant you from seeming weird to them, but rather to save their thinking from the distraction of the surprise of your not jumping in as usual every few seconds. Weirdness is not weird if it is announced ahead of time and grounded in the 'why' of itself.

I mean, you may have to repress, possibly even with a ten-ton psychic hammer, a few thoughts you are pretty sure could change the whole argument and even show you off to be quite the 'choice' choice. But again, you won't die from a conscious hanging back. And you can bestow your irreplaceable thoughts graciously once it's your turn (if they are still relevant).

So how about trying it with a colleague today? And then tomorrow. What if you tried it for a bit longer? And then in a few days you could try it with the person you love most in the world.

In the end it is a decision to trust. To trust the thinker in people. To trust the thinker in yourself.

Go for the frisson.

7. Independent Thinking

Is independent thinking even possible? I love that question. I know why people ask it. Because it isn't. Not in a zero-sum, driven-snow, silo sense. Of course not. And thank goodness. We are absorbent animals. Every single thought we have thought, or heard, or read, or discussed is in us still, turning one thing into another and another into another.

So we are not without influence from the outside. But what we do with that influence is what counts.

We know when we are thinking for ourselves because we are not checking over our shoulder, or probing faces for response, or fearing the price we might pay when the pack leaves without us. We know when our minds are unleashed as themselves. It *feels* different. It *is* different.

So, yes, independent thinking is possible. It is thrilling, in fact, and we were born for it. You could say it is our right. Maybe even our duty.

Recently I was introduced to two Nobel laureates in physics. Generously they asked about my work, and I said that its focus is the question, 'What will it take for people to think for themselves?' They both thought it was an important question but that we would have to start with people younger than six, that humans are born able to develop their innate capacity to think well and independently, but that by the time they are six, it has been beaten out of them. By six it is too late.

I understand their analysis. And if we don't change some crucial things soon in our society as the cradle of the human mind, the physicists will turn out to be right. As you can imagine, though, I am hopeful that the building of thinking environments in the lives of people over six can soon lead both to greater independent thinking by those adults and consequently to the raising of their children free of this early constriction of their minds.

A principal of a primary school said to me recently, 'I am focusing on one thing with this position: to turn school days into thinking days, into think-for-yourself days. I want to see the eyes of the students light up when they realize I mean that. I want the de facto motto of the school to be this question: *What do you really think?*

'I may not get very far. The ferocious force against this campaign is the evaluation/testing fiend that sends teachers crouching into corners of right answers, and students into numbed spirals of performance. So, we'll see. But I want to go down fighting, if nothing else. At least everyone at the school will have had that motto in front of their faces for as long as I last. *What do you really think?*'

I applauded him. And I am following him.

But independent thinking doesn't just happen. Even though our brains are constructed for exactly this. Even though they are loaded with all that spookily folded infrastructure and its 100,000,000,000 x 7,000 neural connections, the brain requires more to produce independent thinking. Things work in context, not in the spotlight.

This quality of thinking arises, as the first eukaryotic cells of life itself in deep-sea vents seem to have, only if the *conditions* are welcoming. In fact, this 'sea vent' dimension of independent thinking is so exciting, so rambunctiously fertile, we need to scoop it up and gaze at it and vow to protect it and proliferate it and never to let it get targeted by lethal injunctions again. The conditions for independent thinking are those ten *behaviours* with each other.

Dr Paul Brown, Faculty Professor at Monarch Business School in Switzerland, explained this to me. He had noticed that these ten behaviours not only work; they work every time.

He said that the reason for this dependable quality of thinking is that generative attention, uncorrupted and sustained, calms the brain's amygdala, the emotional 'control centre' of the brain, producing hormones like serotonin and oxytocin. These hormones then 'bathe' the cortex, the cognitive 'control centre' of the brain, allowing a perfect interplay between these 'approach' hormones and cognition. And because the listener's attention doesn't waver, and we know it won't, the amygdala stays calm, and thought-disturbing hormones like cortisol and adrenaline stay at bay.

Isn't that analysis, like the brain itself, nearly poetry?

The subsequent corroboration of his analysis has been just as beautiful. Particularly elegant is the research by Riana Barnard presented in her dissertation, 'The notions of "attention" and "belief" in coaching for change – a conceptual study' (University of Stellenbosch, Cape Town, South Africa, 2019).

In this work Riana considers the thinking environment in the context of 'advanced perspectives in neurobiology'. So to me it makes sense, is in fact a kind of imperative, to peek at our repetitive behaviour and assess its actual chances of producing fresh thinking in another person, or in ourselves.

To do that maybe we could consider ten questions for a minute, just to ponder what almost all of us are doing when people are thinking for themselves around us. And what is unfolding right in front of us as a result.

These questions will explicate the 'ten components of a thinking environment'. But that is just a conceptual label. Their lived reality is what counts.

And in reality these behaviours are wondrous. They are Nature at work.

I think the human mind is looking for them all of the time.

The Ten Components of a Thinking Environment

ATTENTION

Listening without interruption and with interest in where the person will go next in their thinking

EQUALITY

Regarding each other as thinking peers giving equal time to think

EASE

Discarding internal urgency

APPRECIATION

Noticing what is good and saying it

FEELINGS

Welcoming the release of emotion

ENCOURAGEMENT

Giving courage to go to the unexplored edge of our thinking by ceasing competition as thinkers

INFORMATION

Supplying facts, recognizing social context, dismantling denial

DIFFERENCE

Championing our inherent diversity of identity and thought

INCISIVE QUESTIONS

Freeing the human mind of an untrue assumption lived as true

PLACE

Producing a physical environment – the room, the listener, your body – that says, 'You matter'

8. Component One: Attention

Listening without interruption and with interest in where the person will go next in their thinking

First let me say that if you already know these ten components, I hope this fresh take on them in the form of their implicit questions will deepen your understanding. If they are new to you, I hope you will see immediately how immediate they are, how compelling, how strange, how familiar. And I hope you will ponder which of them is most challenging to live. And decide to live it fully. Even today.

Let's start with the first component's question:

Where is your attention?

That is *the* groundbreaking question. Change where your attention is, and you change where another person's mind is.

Attention *generates* thinking. Think about that. But maybe don't think too hard about it because it will make you feel a bit sick remembering how absent it was from the things you were probably taught about being with people. My guess is that nobody told you that if you give people attention, their minds will start to soar. Nobody said that if you stop giving attention to someone, their minds will slow down and round corners they didn't want to take. Nobody said that if you let a person know that you are wildly interested in what they will think next, they will go brilliantly wild with their own next thoughts. Nobody. Not your parents. Not your teachers. Not your clerics. Not your professional certifiers. Certainly not your bosses. And not even your beloveds. Just about everyone you trusted didn't say that.

But they should have. They should have told you that your continuous, generous attention may be the dearest gift you can give anyone. Or that they can give you. They should have told you that attention of this depth and integrity can produce percipience. Just like that. And its absence can produce stupidity. I am sorry you had to grow up not knowing that. But fortunately, because, as they say, this is the first day of the rest of your life, you can know it from now on.

It matters to know that the bursting-into-life effect of attention is why the promise of no interruption changes everything. In the presence of that promise and its DNA of attention, the human mind laces up, gets on the road, lifts its arms to the heavens and shakes its hair in the early air, exuberant.

And new thoughts, unpredictable connections, *phew*-making insights, razor-edge discernments and I-can't-wait-to-do-them action steps sweep in from nowhere, and a life changes.

Attention.

That glorious force of Nature.

And what does it look like? Not much. Walk into a room where someone is giving attention of this quality and you will think you see one person going on and on and on, and the other just sitting there. Politely, of course. But really not doing much. Certainly nothing worth paying for. And so you hope they are not passing this off as coaching or something. Surely not. You hope it is just an unfortunate person lumbered with a talkathon friend. You walk on.

But stop. Come closer.

Sit down gently for a moment and observe with no rush. Lean in a bit.

I think you will find that the listening person is alive in every pore with 'keep going' messages. These messages beam from the relaxed warmth in their eyes, from their very occasional nod of understanding, from their electrifying stillness, from their absorption in and of every word the person is saying, *and* of what they are not.

Notice the 'thinker', too. They are engaged, palpably. They are moving in and out of new territory, detecting and facing things they haven't before, finding words for elusive impressions and reeling in their own power sometimes for the first time. And suddenly they are quiet for a moment, far longer than allowed in life most places, and then without warning their eyes light up and they laugh. Or they cry. Or they say, 'I see'.

Because they do. And the reason they do is that the listener was different. The listener's attention was in another league altogether. It was fuelled *by* the promise, and it was the fuel *of* the promise. No interruption. Interest. Guaranteed. Finally.

Just before you go, see those other two people? Over there. Yes. Step near for a moment and sit again. They look a lot like the other pair, don't they? One person talking, the other absorbed. But this time, suddenly a flip. The listener talking now, the other absorbed. And even a moment of quiet between them; neither racing to fill it. Then the first talks afresh, the other absorbed, afresh. They smile. They laugh. They order coffee. They start again. No interruption. They decide something. They laugh again.

That was a dialogue, a conversation. Of the finest sort. Life at its best between two people. No gunning down the other's unthought thought. Not scaring the wits out of the other with on-your-mark readiness to pounce. Pure respect. And ebullience.

And a promise: we will not interrupt each other – we will give each other generative attention. The mind wants to work well, to do its own thinking, wherever it is. And with whomever. Even over coffee, just chatting. Life can be like this everywhere.

And the first condition we need in order to think for ourselves as fully and truly as possible wherever we are is this calibre of attention.

The other day, after watching this kind of attention in action for thirty minutes, seeing breakthrough after breakthrough without a single word of input from the listener, a colleague of mine said, 'I have only one word to describe that. *Astonishing*.'

It was. But it shouldn't have been. It should have been the most common thing in the world, hardly worthy of comment.

One day, I hope, it will be.

9. Component Two: Equality

*Regarding each other as thinking peers giving
equal time to think*

Who is your *equal*?

I think about this a lot. It worries me. I'd like to think that I think
that everyone is my equal. I mean that is the right thing for nice
people to think, and I am nice, if nothing else. Also, I am an equality campaigner. I have been marching for decades. Equal rights.
Equal pay. Equal access. Equal opportunity. Equal. Equal. Equal.
And anyway, I practically worship the US Constitution that starts
with a flat-out requirement absolutely to believe that we are all created equal. As of the 14th and 19th Amendments, no buts.

But clearly I don't believe it. How can I tell? I interrupt people. I
apologize when I do it, but I still do it. Not nearly as much as I used
to, and I hate myself when I do do it (which should count for something). But still, I do it. And that act is so loud that all the Main
Street marching bands of America cannot muffle it. I interrupt.
And when I do, it trumpets: 'I am better than you. I matter more.'
It has to mean I do not see you as my equal. Why else would I interrupt you?

I think we have to face it: to interrupt we first must abandon
equality. We must first assume that no matter what the person is
saying, no matter what they are thinking, no matter what they are
about to think, what we want to say is more valuable and in that
moment we matter more than they do. We're better.

And get this nuance: we are not assuming just that our idea is
better; it well may be. We *are* assuming that deep down we deserve
more than they do to speak right this second. If we didn't assume
that, we would listen. We would not speak until they had finished
their thought. We would even stay interested in where they would
go next, and where they would end up.

Right?

Try it. Decide not to interrupt a single person, just for today. You can go back to interrupting tomorrow. You won't forget how. Decide not to interrupt people's talking, of course, but more importantly, decide not to interrupt their *thinking*.

Then notice what you feel. As you listen, you soon begin to will them to stop. Not because they are going on and on pointlessly. But because you now want to speak, and they are behaving as if they matter as much as you do. In this moment they think they are equal to you as a thinking human being. And the emotional part of you that wants desperately to speak can't stand it.

Your rational, smart self, though, knows that of course they *are* as important as you. They do matter equally. They do deserve an uninterrupted turn to speak as much as you do. No matter what they are saying right now. No matter how bored you may be for this second. No matter how Broadway-lights what you want to say will be. No matter how senior you are. They and you matter equally. You know that. We all do.

And when we structure our conversations with each other to express that truth, that we both matter equally, when we promise mutually not to interrupt and to 'share the stage' equally, that infrastructure of equality actually improves the quality of what we then go on to think and say. That's the beauty of it. That is why equality is regarded as a condition for independent thinking, a component of a thinking environment.

But maybe you get off the hook anyway. Maybe you never did believe in equality. Maybe you see the built-in differences of cellular integrity, brain function, hormone strength and the random luck of unequal shelter, food, schooling and parent kindness, and you conclude that there is nothing equal about human beings at all. Story over.

I would agree. In that sense equality is a myth.

But that is not what is at stake here. We can be unequal in all sorts of infrastructural, speed-of-thought, test-acing, child-adored ways, and still be inherently equal as independent thinkers. I have observed too many times to count, and so have too many other people to count, that in the presence of the assumption of equality as human thinkers, people think for themselves better than they do in the presence of interruption and its underlying message of inferiority.

Equality as thinkers regardless of the disparity in our knowledge, the coherence of our chromosomes or the differential in our status is a lithe and limbering force. It helps us think. And its trustiest protector is the promise of no interruption.

Combine attention with this kind of equality, and watch the functional IQs in your circles rise. You won't need to score them. You'll be able to tell. Every thought will have a bit more substance. Every insight more clarity. Each decision more viability. Each question more edge. And each relationship more depth.

Attention and equality.

That is a lot to come from two almost invisible things. And that's just two of ten.

10. *Component Three: Ease*

Discarding internal urgency

Are you acquainted with *ease*? Do you have many moments in a row when you let yourself sigh and settle in and smile from the sweetness of unfrazzled focus, when your brain's vigilant amygdala trusts that there is no threat right now and can scatter serotonin and oxytocin like fairy dust everywhere?

I hope so. But, reluctantly, I wonder. Especially now. A few years ago, before the 'always on' juggernaut culture, there was a chance life held pockets of deep ease for you. You probably even then, though, had to chisel them out of your schedule, and when they finally came round, you had to tiptoe out, closing the door inaudibly behind you, falling back for only the tiniest while into ease's arms. But at least you got there.

Not today. Today we ricochet. And, yes, one wall is the twelve-hour work day. Yes, one is the stand-up, ten-minute meeting. One is the caffeine. One is the copy-everyone-in-to-cover-yourself fall-back. But those are the fight-for-your-life usuals. And at least you can see them and, should you be courageous, protest them, and with a bit of influence, replace them.

Not these, though. These are the resolution-resistant eaters of ease that prey on our need to be liked, our need to feel in the know, our need to feel at the centre, our craving to be pricked one more time in order to feel the creep of relief because we solved the mystery of who said what, who thinks what, who loves me. Those jerk-us-around consumers of ease are the commoditizers of our attention we call digital push notifications. They are the persuasion predators. I will talk much more about this in chapter 24. But here consider that their very *raison d'être* is to tell us where to put our attention. They crash in on purpose. They interrupt us on purpose. They get to control us. They can suck out our ease.

So we have to learn this, get this, stare this ruthlessly down. We have to see what is happening to us, notification by notification, checking by checking, scrolling by scrolling, tapping by tapping, posting by posting, and restore our natural loathing of these faux emergencies, our giant indignation, our irrepressible resolve to end it.

We need to face this ease-acidifying creature so hard we nearly burst.

And when we do, when we finally do, we can take charge of our lives again and sit. Still. We can breathe then. We can notice the world. We can notice our own hearts beating. We can notice our friend's eyes wondering. We can notice our child's silence piercing. We can let the nearly annihilated neurons of ease fire again, one, then two, then two trillion. Until we are back.

Ease is a kind of womb. Thought, invulnerable because calmed, emerges there, and plays and bends and stretches until it reshapes its very self and settles into 'Thank you, yes, that's it.'

But when there is no ease, when there is only the cacophony of 'look at me', thought seeks shelter and leaves only a detective's outline of itself on the floor.

We were born to remember ease. We were raised to forget it.

So if it is permission you need, consider it granted. You can reinstate ease as your personal culture, as your default, as your canvas of life. You can insist on ease. And only then can you think for yourself fully, blissful, barely able to remember when big data legions led your life and you were so woven into their arsenal of distraction, interruption and conformity you praised them with your allegiance and your cortisol and the desiccating of your magnificent cortex, and you hardly noticed. Then you can laugh because it is over; and where you put your attention is now entirely a conscious, not controlled, choice.

Thinking for yourself depends on it. And so does your easeful, catalytic way of being with others so that they can think for themselves, too. And so does every minute of every relationship. None is expendable or exempt. None. Each is slipping away as I speak. And each will require ease to be rescued.

Attention, too, depends on ease. So does equality.

11. *Component Four: Appreciation*

Noticing what is good and saying it

Why is appreciation rare, still?

Baffling, isn't it? Mozart was praised for his piano prowess when he was three, and look what happened. By the age of eight he had composed (*composed!*) a symphony. Have you heard it? No. 1, K 16. Download it immediately.

And consider this, too: praise, appreciation, expressions of respect – all develop human thinking. They unwrap confidence and let it saturate talent and will and buds of ability. You know this. Every time someone mentions a quality they admire in you, you do even better at just about everything for a while. And you feel good. And you think better.

And that's the point. That good-feeling phenomenon is a good-thinking phenomenon. So says the chemistry at least. Appreciate someone and, as with attention, the hormones in their brain change. Oxytocin, serotonin and dopamine dash around their cortex; and before they know it, they think better and better. We have noticed this repeatedly in all of our work.

So what's the problem? Why don't we do it more? It's not that difficult. We can just notice what is good and say it. That's it.

In fact, the next time you are with a human being, anywhere at all, notice something you respect about them, or like about them, or just think is a plus for that moment, and tell them. Even strangers. Their day will change, and when they start to think about something, they'll be better at it.

I was walking up the stairs to the room where I would be lecturing that day, and someone passed me, saying, 'We like it when you are here, Nancy.' Well, you would have thought an entire string ensemble had struck up on the lawn to play in my honour with fireworks to follow, for as much as that passing comment did for my day and my thinking.

It doesn't take much to change a brain.

And you know, just about the best way you can appreciate someone is to ask them this powerful, disarmingly simple question: 'What do *you* think?'

That act says ten (at least) appreciative things at once. You can guess what those things are, starting with, 'I respect you as a thinker.' You can't get much more appreciative than that. And in the face of that appreciation, a brain can work better than it has in ages.

Why? Mark McMordie, business coach, mindfulness expert and co-author of *Mindfulness for Coaches*, says that it is because appreciation creates psychological safety. And that is what we need in order to risk developing and expressing what we think. What we *really* think.

So let's once and for all bin the ludicrous lore, imposed on us all aeons ago probably to keep us subservient and unable to think for ourselves, that appreciating people is dangerous. Let's notice that not appreciating them is.

And by the way, the reason we agree to dangle from the drool of push notifications is that we crave appreciation. We seek the likes. And the likes of us. So I figure that when appreciation is our everyday culture, the very air we breathe, those jaws won't have a chance even to open.

And we will be smarter as a result.

12. *Component Five: Feelings*
Welcoming the release of emotion

What do you do when someone suddenly expresses *feelings*? If they cry, or get a bit ragey, let's say. Or tremble. What then? How long can you listen to emotion without trying to remember the phone number of a therapist?

I've seen and heard a lot of feeling in my listening life. And I have yet to see anything but good from it. It seems only to heal and to allow the mind to work less impeded. Unexpressed emotion, on the other hand, seems to block both thought and health. So I am unbothered when people cry or say how angry or scared they are. I am pleased, actually.

I used to wonder how long a person needs to cry about, say, early childhood things. And I have yet to learn how much release is enough to restore healing and clear thinking. Two hundred hours of crying on one incident, as touted by one teacher of exhaustive emotional release, seems a bit much to me; and I have not seen impressive results from that. But two hours may well be too little. And even that is way more than our cultures can contemplate. So I just relax in the face of emotion and trust that the person will 'self-regulate' if I don't get nervous and stop them, or become fanatical and keep them going.

The main thing is that society is completely weird about all of this and jumps out of its skin with the first undabbed tear. Although I notice these days a bit less rigidity about feelings among people who have accurate information about the benefits of emotional release, we really do need to change this societal aversion to feelings, starting with every newborn, toddler, child, teenager and adult we know. Spread the word: feelings are fine. In the right places, of course. And that takes some discernment. But we can figure that out. We don't freak out when people exercise, but we don't allow it in the middle of the aisle at the opera either. So this big change should not be hard.

Most important is that feelings are so interwoven with thinking that to allow one and not the other is to diminish both. We can listen to words and we can listen to tears. It is all the same thing. I know that at the moment the world of brain talk is full of the separation of these two systems. But that will pass soon enough, just as almost all efforts at human compartmentalization have. Life is everything all at once. Even space is stuff that hugs us. Life is one lavish act of touching. Thinking and feeling are no exceptions. So we can rejoice.

And when someone is thinking along and starts to cry, let's just be glad they felt psychologically safe enough with us to do that. And then watch the fresh thinking that follows. And the bright eyes that say so.

As you know, I often ask, when I am listening to a person a bit formally (i.e. not over coffee) and they have said they can't think of anything else, 'What more do you think, *or feel*, or want to say?' Or a version of that. If people have had some waves of thinking they usually can have more, and sometimes the next wave is full of feeling as well as insight.

The point is that release of feelings should always be a choice. It is not all of the picture, and it does not need to be the sole target of our attention or skill in listening. And feelings are not usually a reliable guide for intelligent decision-making (although they are in practice the root of most people's decisions).

But release of emotion does help us think better and more fully for ourselves. You can probably remember times when you expressed your feelings with people who listened, who did not silence or interrupt you, or inject their own feelings. Most likely you were able then to think more calmly, and more clearly.

The principle I use to sum up the component of feelings in a thinking environment is not just a quip: crying can make you smarter.

It really can.

13. Component Six: Encouragement

Giving courage to go to the unexplored edge of our thinking by ceasing competition as thinkers

All the components of a thinking environment talk to each other, influencing each other, enriching each other, holding each other accountable. We learn more about one by hearing the 'conversations' it has with the others. This is particularly true of 'encouragement'.

In a thinking environment 'encouragement' returns to its literal meaning: to give courage. It gives us courage to go to the unfamiliar edge of our thinking. In order to do that we have to trust that there will be no competition between us as thinkers. We have to champion each other's *mutual* excellence as thinkers. And so you could say that the component of encouragement converses steadily with the component of equality.

If I promise you that I will not interrupt you because I respect you as a thinker as much as I respect myself, you will venture further in your thinking than if you sense my impatience to improve your thinking right now because I already know that mine is better.

So to offer each other the component of encouragement is to abandon competition between us as bold thinkers so that we do not abandon our bold thinking before it emerges.

Life loves the best thought but cares not a whit about who thought it.

14. *Component Seven: Information*

Supplying facts, recognizing social context,
dismantling denial

Isn't 'information' just too boring a thing for this scintillating 'components' cache?

Not for a second. In fact, information as it affects (and effects) human independent thinking is captivating.

I am not a data geek. I am wary, in fact, of the unregulated big data world that is stalking humanity. My bewitchment with information is different. It is with the mind's hunger to understand, 'its desire to know' as Aristotle said. And that kind of knowing seems to require three things: 1) supplying the facts, 2) seeing the social collective context and 3) dismantling denial.

The maddening irony is that even as we desire to know, we swerve from the knowing.

Too often, for example, we gather up only the facts that fit our preferred view. Or we withhold facts and data from others, perhaps for fear of losing the power we have when only we have that information.

Similarly, we sit in a room full of information but do not honour it. This information is, in the words of my South African colleague Althea Banda-Hansmann, our 'social collective context'. This is the overlapping histories and their imposed identities we bring into any room, along with their experiences of trauma and triumph, of assumptions and truth, of our giving in and of our rising up. This social context is also the current society's still-institutionalized version of these histories, as well as our current living of and in them. It is all there when we gather. But seldom is this form of information acknowledged, much less factored in to our thinking. So, to ensure independent thinking we must see and, in appropriate ways, acknowledge, this social collective context that is a mighty form of information.

And that requires us to come to terms with denial. We human beings, while desiring to know, also deny like mad. We deny not just our overlapping social contexts, but equally our individual perceptions. These challenging perceptions are there on the road with us, but we pull out and pass them, hardly waving. If I were to ask you one of my favourite questions, 'What are you not facing that is right in front of your face?', you would know. But most likely you would immediately cram it back into its Houdini trunk. And sit on it. And try to think from there.

But that is no position for thinking. If we want truly to think for ourselves, we need to know about denial.

Knowing about denial, however, does not dismantle it. We have to be brave to do that. In order to look that information squarely in the face and face it down, we have to want our real selves more than we want our imagined ones.

I think that is thrilling. I think that this component of information, seen as the complex creature it is, is almost spellbinding. It allows for clear, shaken-out thinking to take place. In its presence there can be no lies to muck up the perception and the conclusion. There can be no closing off of the context we inhabit. There can be no running away from the presence present.

Importantly, too, information prevents adoration, one of the most dangerous forces against the independent human mind. The choice to see no flaws, the choice to justify every inconsistency or contradiction by saying it isn't happening or by sewing in an interpretation that allows it to fit the dogma of the adored. We see adoration in the same-stepping rallies of worshippers of any sort: of politicians, fashion, deity, battle, wealth. When reality does not fit the narrative and the narrative is substituting for our own stories of meaning and purpose and significance, we worship. We ignore facts. We term 'fake' what is real. We have stopped thinking for ourselves. We have stopped thinking, full stop.

So I would catapult information to the top of what sings, and moves the earth, and matters.

I would ask many times a day, what is real? What uncomfortable actualities can we uncover today to fill in the picture more accurately? What is right in front of us? What new land can we traverse to arrive where the veracity lies? How brazenly can we seek a wider truth when it disquiets our narrow own?

These answers depend on our inside integrity. And they require our listening. They require the promise that we will not interrupt, no matter where the search leads, no matter what it discovers, no matter what of our testament has to collapse for the discoveries to be invited in.

Tell me what you really think. Tell me what is really happening. Tell me what you have actually found. And I'll tell you. We won't interrupt. We will learn and change and build together.

Information is that much a friend, that much a wand.

15. Component Eight: Difference

Championing our inherent diversity of identity and thought

How much *difference* can you stand?

Most of us are committed to it. Just about every company, firm, practice and organization flaunts 'diversity and inclusion' as one of their core values. Some even have a whole department dedicated to it. Some people even believe in it. All good.

But when it comes down to it, who are your neighbours? Who worships with you? Who advises you? Who joins you on the streets holding up the other side of your placard? Who attends your school? Whom do you secretly pray your children will never marry?

Valuing difference is a big job. It takes more than a department or a sermon or a march to embed it. We live in cultures; and cultures resist difference. They are set up to draw a circle around sameness and close it with a secret handshake.

We think we like it. We think we can relax when everyone with us is the same. We think we are safe. And some evolutionists would tell you that tribes, by definition closed to 'others', are the way *sapiens* survived. But others just as erudite would disagree. It is exactly because we could adapt to difference, they would say, that we could survive change. Either theory works well enough. But neither helps much.

Difference is all there is. There is no such thing as same. That's the curious thing. All this clubbiness, all this we/they super-construction in our rituals and rites, all this being-an-exclusive-member-of drive we learn as we grow up – none of it is real. Inside every group there is so much difference we would drown trying to slosh through it all. So we pretend. Here is your medallion. Now you are one of us. We are all the same. Thank goodness.

Translate that to mean not just that we dress the same and

holiday the same and vote the same. Translate it to mean 'we think the same'. That is the danger. Never mind the outfits and the oaths. It is the sameness of thought that weakens the human mind.

How much danger are you in? How thoroughly have you agreed to think like everyone else, or to pretend to? In fact, can we-are-the-same even be measured? And if it can, what is a lethal dose?

The best way I know of to test our relationship with difference is to listen to someone who looks or talks or lives differently from us and whose ideas appal us. See if you can locate someone like that (it won't be hard because they are all of the people immediately out-side your circles) and engage them in conversation about an issue you are secretly sure they are wrong about. Tell them you want to learn from them and to understand why they think the way they do about the issue. And see how long you can listen without want-ing to strangle them or at least interrupt them mid-syllable in order to set them straight.

Notice your heartbeat. Notice your frown.

Difference is often so deeply threatening we cannot bear to lis-ten to it. Much less embrace it. We cannot bear to imagine that we might be wrong and they might be right and, heaven forbid, at least as good in every way as we are. Or better.

The culprit here is an unavoidable sequence of childhood. When people are brought up to fear difference, especially difference of thought, they are easier to control. And society adores control.

Society is also cunning. And before we as babies have quite com-pleted making all the brain we need to scrutinize society and its controls before we sign up to them, we find ourselves sliding down its glaciers cut by its regolith and moraine, having been pushed tri-umphantly by the people at the top whom we trusted with our lives. Such is the delay in our ability to think for ourselves and the unfortunate things we have to go through until we can.

Nevertheless, now we can. And now we must. Our lives depend on our comfort with difference because difference is all there is, and because our brains need that comfort in order to venture into unexplored territory and come forth with the great ideas we need in order to be deeply happy, and in order for society to recognize its multiple overlapping social contexts and wiggle itself loose from prejudice, narcissism and war. And from gargantuan systems of finance and power that appear to be melting the planet. We need to adore difference so that we can all finally, in fact, be the same in the only sense that matters: as human beings. And what magnificence that sameness is.

So how about we walk across the road and listen? And soon ask to be listened to, too. And promise never to interrupt. Only to learn. And eventually to respect?

And then, who knows?

To love?

16. Component Nine: Incisive Questions

Freeing the human mind of an untrue
assumption lived as true

What is an 'incisive' question?

You already know. We all do. We know what an incisive question is because we form them and use them silently, imperceptibly, every day. They are the way we break through when we are stuck. They are the way we feel better when we feel bad. And they are the way we occasionally draw gasps from people when their thinking breaks through because we ask them a perfectly formed incisive question. Nature, I think, outdid herself with this set of mutations a staggering amount of time ago.

That is what we observe. The gear to form an incisive question seems to come with the human cognitive package. It is that universal. And it is elegant.

I learned this at lunch one day. If you have read *Time to Think*, you may remember this story. I was with my new friend, Penny, in Middleburg, Virginia. The restaurant was filled with quiet women dressed in understated outfits, most with pearls. My mother would have loved it. *I* loved it, for that matter.

Penny and I were talking about her life. She had said that she wanted to work less and earn more and spend more time with her family. I was listening (those were my early days of not interrupting). When she got to the end of her thinking, I asked her a question. And she erupted. She shouted (truly), 'Stop right there! Stop!' She folded her napkin. I thought she might be going to get up and leave.

'What were you thinking,' she said, still way too loud for a place with so many pearls, 'just before you asked me that question? Just before. What was going through your mind that made you ask it?'

I glanced apologetically at the frowns around the room and whispered to Penny (thinking in vain, as I always do when someone is embarrassingly loud, that if I speak quietly, they will, too; it never works), 'I have no idea, Penny. I can't even remember what the question was.'

Penny said, 'Well, I was talking about wanting to make changes in my job and then said that my husband would be angry if I upset my boss; and you said, "If you knew that you can handle anything your husband might do or say, what would you propose to your boss?"'

'And bingo, I had an idea of how I could restructure my job. Just like that, out of nowhere. And it happened just after you asked me that question.'

'Well good,' I said, 'I'm glad.'

'No,' she said. 'I don't want you to be glad. I want to know what *caused* you to think of that question. I figure something must have been going on in your head that made you think of it. So what was it?'

'I have no idea,' I said.

She put her napkin back in her lap. 'Well, try,' she said.

I did. It took me seven years.

I am not always that slow at figuring things out. And when you hear an incisive question, it doesn't seem that sophisticated. 'If you knew *x*, how would you do *y*?' Seven years?

Actually, more. More like seventeen because all of its exquisite innards work so mellifluously together it is almost like separating throat from trill to get a good peek at it, and that takes time. Nature is like that. You can be standing right in front of a thing and not see it. And then all at once your mind walks around the block a few times while you are not looking and suddenly stops, transfixed by the very mystery that was in plain sight all along. Seeing is a big deal.

In fact, when you don't interrupt (and the person thinking knows you won't), you can 'see' people forming this kind of question for themselves. Sometimes right out loud. Like this:

I want to speak up more in meetings. But new team members should defer to others. They really should. Or should they? Maybe they shouldn't. Maybe they should offer their thinking precisely because they are new and are still able to see things from new angles. Well, if I knew that, I'd speak up. In fact, I will. Tomorrow morning.

And they do.

Or sometimes people form an incisive question without saying all of that but implying it in the outcome.

I'd like to speak up more in meetings. But new people should defer to others. Actually, forget it, I am going to speak up in meetings, starting tomorrow.

That 'sudden' decision to speak up had to have been arrived at through a true liberating alternative to 'new people should defer to others'. And that liberating assumption ('new people should offer their thinking *precisely because* they are new and are still able to see things from new angles') had to have been considered by the brain in a way that would embed it sufficiently to become a credible new reality.

The brain needs a question for that job. The brain loves questions. And the only question construct I know of that does not set off the brain's resistance to the new assumption is exactly that hypothetical construct we call an incisive question.

So here in one sentence (albeit dense) is what this life-restoring kind of question seems to do:

An incisive question, through a playful hypothetical construct, replaces an untrue limiting assumption with a true liberating one, and connects it to a desired outcome.

And here is why (even denser):

The key block *to a desired outcome is an* untrue limiting assumption lived as true *that can be removed only by replacing it with a true liberating assumption inserted into a playful (because hypothetical) question using the subjunctive tense.*

E.g. if you knew x, how would you do y? The mind can play inside that construct. And in playing, it embeds the new true assumption and decides on actions and/or changes its feelings. Everything.

The brain likes to play, not obey. And the incisive question construct lets it do that. Playful because hypothetical. Wonderful to know.

We will explore later in some depth the road to these magical questions. But for now, just begin to notice them. Incisive questions are all around you. And they are in you. Most new ideas come from them.

And most joy.

17. Component Ten: Place

Producing a physical environment – the room, the listener, your body – that says, 'You matter'

Do you know your *place*?

When a place is a place where you can think truly for yourself, it is probably saying back to you, 'You matter.' This message comes from three sources at once: the room, the listener and your body.

First consider the room.

We sit in a room and wonder why we can't think so well. We gather with others in a room and wonder why they can't think so well. We chalk it up to idiocy, laziness or infuriating counter-dependence. Or politics. Or overwork. Or periods. Or time.

But for the life of us we don't look around and see what the room itself is saying to everyone there. It is talking a mile a minute, but our ignorance of the power of 'place' mutes that.

Is it the dirty mugs, the fluorescent light, the dead philodendron? Is it the charcoal carpet and the black-and-white zigzaggy wall-paper? Is it the status-is-everything boardroom leather chairs and bevelled glass table? Is it branded pencils lined up like soldiers?

Their messages are all the same. 'You don't matter.' And then they elaborate, 'No one has thought about you in particular before arriving here; nothing has been done to welcome *you*, to account for *your* particular needs or cultures or personalities, to anticipate the value of *your* participation. You are here, but this place doesn't care about that. So sit down.'

And the listener?

You could argue that this aspect of the component of place contains the most electrifying and life-critical feature of a thinking environment. The listener. The listener is the force. *The* force. Without the listener we don't have a thinking environment. For years I thought that place was only the room or space we occupy.

Then I realized that the condition of our bodies also must say to us as thinker, 'You matter.' Only recently did I see that place is most of all the listener, who *with almost every breath* says, 'You matter.' I'm not sure how I missed that. I console myself that the obvious is nearly always unseen. I now wonder if I should put 'place' first among the components. It has been last for decades. I best not go there.

What specifically matters about this listener aspect of place are the eyes and face. Here's how: the thinker is thinking and talking and looking intermittently at the listener. During all of that the listener's eyes are on the eyes of the thinker, picking up micro signals in the thinker's eyes and face. Simultaneously, the listener's own eyes and face are responding accurately by the second to those signals.

In the moment when the thinker looks back at the listener, they register the degree of accuracy in the listener's response to their signals. They see that response in the thinker's eyes and face. And here's the bombshell: the degree of accuracy of the listener's response to the signals may determine the level of psychological safety for the thinker. The more accurate the listener's response, the more convincingly the thinker reads, 'You matter.' And the better they think.

So it could be said that the definition of truly *generative* attention, the thing that makes generative attention generative, is *the perfectly calibrated eye-and-face response by the listener to the micro signals in the eyes and face of the thinker*. The more accurate, the more generative.

The listener's accurate response to the thinker's changes seems to raise the quality of attention to a generative zenith. And even more extraordinary things seem to happen for the thinker because of it.

The listener's eyes and face are place. Yes.

And your body?

When you sit down to think, and the body you are in is anything but a statement that 'you matter', some part of your thinking apparatus knows that. It mumbles for the whole time you are thinking. It wants to be respected as if it, too, were a thinker. Because it is.

But we act as if it were hardly there. And as if it doesn't have a thing to do with how well we think.

It does, though. Obviously, our brains are in our bodies, and thus depend on body chemistry in order to work. Too much sugar, sluggish brain. Too much wheat, compliant brain. Too much artificial stuff, fearful brain. Too much alcohol and drug stuff, collapsed brain.

But the impact of our bodies on thinking goes beyond this chemistry question. When we try to think inside a body we disrespect, it can hear only, 'You don't matter.' And that assumption practically anaesthetizes the cortex.

The body, then, is the place where we think, not only because it contains our brains, but also because it tells us whether we matter.

What to do?

Consider these questions.

About the room:

What are three things you can do before your next meeting so that when people arrive they feel, just from the room, that they matter?

About the listener:

How can you communicate to your listener the importance of their keeping their eyes on your eyes so that their eyes and their face respond accurately to the micro signals of change in your thinking?

About your body:

What one thing do you know you need to do so that your body can say to you, 'You matter'?

A Virtual Place

And when your place is virtual? Can it work? Can Zoom, for example, be a thinking environment?

Yes. With intriguing caveats.

The ten components of a thinking environment improve a virtual place significantly. Particularly for meetings. And even one-to-one virtual sessions are of much higher quality if they are as close to a thinking environment as possible. People are often rapturous about their online thinking environment meetings and conversations because they are such a wonderful improvement.

Equally and interestingly, it is not yet certain whether virtual meetings or individual sessions can be fully nuanced thinking environments. And, as of this writing, we are researching a particular distinction: the difference between 'genuine attentiveness' and 'generative attention'.

Groups seem almost always able to achieve 'genuine attentiveness' on virtual video platforms, and with excellent results, *if* they agree to keep the promise of no interruption, to establish rounds of equal turns and to adopt as many of the components of a thinking environment as possible.

But one-to-one sessions that rely on more than genuine attentiveness for their power may be a different story in a virtual place. These sessions require 'generative attention' to achieve cutting-edge independent thinking. And as we have seen above, generative attention seems to require a particularly high level of signalling and response between the eyes and faces of the thinker and listener. And some platforms can inhibit this level of refined connection.

The platform may, for example, require the eyes of the listener to be on the computer's camera and not on the eyes and face of the thinker. And so the micro signals are lost to the listener in their lower periphery. Also, unpredictably but not un-often, an erratic broadband connection can skew the thinker's face and words and further reduce the refinement of the listener's processing of the thinker's signals. And of course the digital connection can drop altogether.

All of these are interruptions. Even the threat of these occurrences acts as an interruption. This would seem to mean that on screen we cannot keep the promise of no interruption. And that should mean that superb one-to-one thinking sessions on screen are doomed. But they aren't. Far from it. People describe their on-screen thinking sessions as brilliant, invaluable, shimmering. Rapture again.

This puzzled me. But then I thought about this: on screen the promise of no interruption is broken, yes. But not by the listener. It is broken by the platform. And it is the listener's promise, not the platform's, that ignites the thinker's mind. It is the thinker's trust in that human promise that allows them to claim their own intelligence and fly. And although this means that one of the three aspects of the component of place – the room – is deeply compromised, the most important aspect – the listener – holds steady and perhaps does 'double duty' to make up significantly for the interruptive room.

There is still a loss of thinking, of course. But on-screen sessions are almost always stunning. For some people those thinking-environment on-screen sessions are richer than their non-thinking-environment in-person lives.

So our big question is: does truly generative attention require a physical reality?

We shall see.

Ironically, but maybe not surprisingly, one-to-one audio sessions, because they avoid this visual processing interruption, can work better sometimes than the video experience. To some they seem more 'real'. To some, even safer as well. A version of this phenomenon may explain why a session if we are blind can work so well.

Also not surprisingly, both video and audio thinking environments seem to work better if the people involved have experienced a thinking environment in person first, preferably many times. Then online it is as if they draw on their 'limbic memory' of those in-person times to manufacture imagined levels of connection in the virtual presence. This 'limbic memory' may then help compensate for the reduced precision of thinker/listener signal exchange.

But regardless, a thinking environment is both a must and a gift for online thinking together. Every interaction benefits, usually dramatically.

I think that this on-screen success illustrates how hungry the human mind is for a thinking environment to help it soar. It will make the very best use of whatever amount of uninterrupted generative human attention it can get.

In the end it comes down to this: Place matters. Because you do.

18. A Positive Philosophical Choice: Revisited

There is another important dimension of the ten components. They bring to life a particular philosophy of human nature. I mention this because one's chosen philosophy of human nature is vital. It determines where we focus. And our focus determines where we go.

As seasoned motorbikers know, and as Matthew Tomlin, one of the best, explained to me, 'On a motorbike you arrive where you focus. So you'd better be focused ahead.'

To produce fine independent thinking we need to do that, too. We need to focus 'ahead' on our inherent capacity for 'good'. We need to focus on our capacity for respect, intelligence, learning, kindness, creativity, depth, love, feeling, integrity and delight. We need not to be distracted by our capacity for 'bad': disdain, stupidity, stagnation, violence, derivation, superficiality, hate, numbness, mendacity and gloom.

We do have both capacities, of course, inherently. And for many years I had maintained (hoped?) that humans could be regarded as *inherently* good, *entirely*. I had asserted that bad human behaviour was not inherent, that it was *entirely* a result of experience and the untrue assumptions it leaves behind.

I can no longer embrace that view. The science that recognizes occasional inborn brain distortions that can produce the 'bad' in human behaviour is too strong to wish away.

I think we can, however, assert that our capacity for 'good' is of a higher order than our capacity for 'bad' and, therefore, merits our focus. I say 'higher order' because the science of the brain suggests that only the 'good' *feeds* human development. The 'bad' limits, even derails, human development. For example, when the human is born, the brain arrives not fully formed and needs further 'processing'. That 'processing', as it turns out, is a form of the 'good'. Key in this is sustained generative attention supported by the other components of a thinking environment.

In contrast, no newborn requires the 'bad' in order to develop its brain. In fact, in the presence of the 'bad', including the absence of generative attention and of the other components, the infant brain can arrest development, producing over time a stunted emotional system, and ultimately even sociopathic behaviour.

So we could say that, yes, both the potential for 'bad' and the potential for 'good' exist innately in the human being. But because the 'good' feeds human development and the 'bad' starves it, the potential for 'good' in us outweighs in impact and power the potential for 'bad'.

The choice, then, to focus on the 'good' matters because it changes the way we listen. You know when someone says something that irks you? And they continue. Then they irk you more. They say more. Irk turns to anger. Soon you aren't hearing a thing they are saying. You're not sure you even like them any more.

But if you're lucky, you remember the 'positive philosophical choice'. You pull yourself together. You reflect that this person has an inherent higher order of capacity for good. You move back from the any-second-now superimposition of yourself on to them. You start to take in again what they are saying. You note that they have progressed a bit. You get interested in where they are headed. You listen.

The positive philosophical choice, the discipline of returning to the human's capacity for 'good', can save us from our petty, and destructive, forays into dismissiveness.

This discipline works in groups, too. In fact, in groups we are even more likely to dabble in self-righteous judgement and focus on the person's capacity for the 'bad' as we listen. It is as if we unilaterally farm out to the others in the group the responsibility for being a thinking environment, and we take a spin in their parked criticism. And even if we don't actually air any of that, our attention has left the premises. The person speaking can tell.

This is the moment when the positive philosophical choice rescues a thinking environment. We refocus. We zoom in on the person's vast capacity for 'good'. We get interested in where they will go with their thinking. They pick up speed and quality. We notice. We breathe.

I think that if we want to produce the best thinking in human beings, including ourselves, we must, as we listen, decide reiteratively to see this higher order of 'good' in the person in front of us.

We must make a 'positive philosophical choice'.

The human's vast capacity for 'good' is a worthy mantra. For the sake of our thinking, I propose we return to it every chance we get.

19. *But Is It Always Good?*

'All fine,' said one of my students recently, 'humans may be domin-
antly good beings; but do we know that *independent* thinking is
necessarily *good* thinking?'

I love this question, too. I think about it a lot.

We need to start by defining good thinking.

What do you think good thinking is? When you figure it out, ask
a friend or two. And then a couple of not-friends, people whose
thinking drives you mad. See if at least the ballpark of what good
thinking is is the same for all of you.

I asked some of my friends and then some of my hard-to-bear
not-friends. We were surprisingly close. For sure no one said, 'Good
thinking starts with obedience to an unexamined, externally
imposed, half-erroneous, emotionally charged, narcissist-endorsed
perspective and leads to similarly ignorant and emotionally hijacked
conclusions.' No one thought that. That was a relief. You would not
necessarily have predicted that by looking around the world these
days.

I think that good thinking starts with a factual or logical premise.
It then searches for *all* the accurate, relevant information available.
It considers that. And then, free of upset or gimmicks of persuasion
(like nicknames and labels or vague references to authoritative
sources – more on these 'persuasion' tactics in chapter 25), builds a
conclusion from that informed premise.

Let's say for the moment that that definition of good thinking is
valid. Does a thinking environment, then, with its attention-imbued
promise not to interrupt, with its component of information, its
encouraging freedom from competition, its fundamental equality
of turn, its ease, its knowledge of the starring and ensnaring role of
untrue limiting assumptions and its championing of difference,
ensure good thinking? Almost always, in my experience.

Even when we are listening to the people we hate, their thinking improves and so does ours when we provide these conditions.

I think that is pretty exciting.

But let's pretend that we can't be sure that a thinking environment will inevitably engender good thinking. Let's say that sometimes even when elegantly produced these conditions for thinking aren't sufficient for a person's independent thinking to be completely good *immediately*. What then?

That doesn't worry me. For one thing, we can see right in front of us that their thinking is better than it was under conditions of interruption, co-option and control. And I have seen people's independent thinking on one day improve some the next day and more the next, if they experience the same optimal conditions.

That is the key here. The *conditions*. Often people will say that they are thinking for themselves when actually they don't have a prayer of doing that because the conditions are corrupting it by the second.

I also have seen people's self-respect grow because they knew they would not be interrupted and that the person listening was truly interested in where they would go next with their thinking. That had formidable power to bestow exactly the courage to examine their premises and conclusions ruthlessly. That greater self-respect led to better and better thinking.

It just sometimes takes a bit of time. We are not going to leap in a single bound over the last umpteen millennia of obedience and think-for-me defaults, and in one sitting produce always-good thinking of our own. It will take a few goes. But not as many as you'd think. We humans are poised to reclaim our birthright to independent thinking, if we know we can trust the conditions.

So that leaves us at this sunny juncture: dependably independent thinking becomes, sooner than you'd imagine, good thinking. Therefore, the decision to produce it in ourselves and in others matters like mad.

PART TWO

Understanding Interruption

20. Sources of Interruption

If you were to ask people what they think interruption is, they would say something like: crashing into someone's sentence; 'tailgating' someone's sentence; finishing someone's sentence for them. Or they may, unusually, recognize that interruption is also answering someone's question before they have finished formulating it, preventing, of course, the refinement and precision of the question and the usefulness of the answer.

Right. But not entirely. The point is not the interruption just of the person's sentence or question. The point is the interruption of their *thinking*. When we interrupt people's sentences, we interrupt their thinking. Realizing that can be sobering. When we see interruption as breaking only into people's words, we do it and scoot off. When we recognize it as demolishing their thinking, we stop. Or at least pause.

And that is what matters here: interruption as the demolition of people's thinking.

Interruption of thinking comes from a number of sources. These are the most pervasive:

Ourselves
Others
Occurrences
Assumptions
Systems

When we begin to see these five everywhere-things as sources of interruption, we have new power to curtail their impact. Seeing, as we have seen, is everything.

Ourselves

First, as usual, we have to start with ourselves. In this case, we are our first and most deadly interrupter. We interrupt our own thinking. We do this by not seeing ourselves as thinkers and, therefore, by not valuing our own thinking. And so, we interrupt ourselves as soon as we get started. We just stop. We defer to others to think for us. And they oblige with relish. It is perverse in the extreme. But almost all of us do it almost all of the time.

In previous chapters I have talked about the importance of our reclaiming our right and capacity to think for ourselves, and we will look at that again later.

Drawing on all of that I will say here only that deciding to start seeing ourselves as thinkers, and to take proper and frequent time to think for ourselves, is a way, possibly the only way, to subdue this most debilitating primary source of interruption, ourselves.

You can start now. The very next time you find yourself deferring to someone else's thinking, stop. Then ask yourself:

What do I think here?

Take your time and your turn to work it out, and to say it. Your thinking self will be grateful that you interrupted its worst interrupter: you.

Others

Second, other people interrupt us. So far we have explored the blatant ways people interrupt us. The three examples above – exploding into, tailgating and finishing people's sentences – are the most common ones, built destructively into the very way we live.

But there are more wily ways others interrupt us, acts never recognized as interruption. Here are three:

People pay a lot for this source of interruption. People ask others for the free version of it every day. People give it unasked for every day. It is not only unrecognized as interruption of thinking; it is sanctioned as enhancement of it.

It works this way: we let a person think and talk only until we have thoughts for them. Then we tell them. Telling them without invitation long before the person has thought fully for themselves is interruption enough. But here's the killer: we tell them our thoughts in the 'language of advice'. We say things like, 'You could . . . You should . . . I would propose that you . . . You'd do well to . . . If I were you, I would . . .', 'Do this, think that, get on with it just as I say.'

That 'language of advice' is itself an interruption of the person's independent thinking. When we use that language, we are requiring the person to think like us, in essence to *become* us. So the person's mind becomes defensive. People resist having to think just like someone else. This requirement is demeaning; it is diminishing of the self. And so, what is offered in the language of advice is usually only partially heard and often rejected, sometimes out of hand.

But if instead we use the language of experience – 'I discovered that . . . In my experience, I have found that . . .' – or the language of information – 'the law says that . . . research is showing that . . . so far the facts here are that . . .' – or even, 'if I were in your situation, I would . . .', the person engages readily, accepting bits, rejecting bits, questioning bits. They keep thinking for themselves. They keep their own mind. They have not been required to become us.

Advice always did ring strangely, didn't it? The recipient always did seem slightly to disappear in the face of the advice-giver, didn't they, no matter how much they thanked the adviser at the end? I've for ages wondered about that. Now I think I understand it: the language of advice invisibilizes the advised. It requires them to abandon their own self and to conform. It is an interruption of independent thinking.

This interruption is grey-toned. But it is there all around us. And I think it accounts for the appalling strike rate of advice-givers.

According to Dr Thomas G. Plante (*Psychology Today*, 15 July 2014), 'advice giving usually doesn't work, and often completely backfires'. People want to think for themselves more than they want to think as someone else. Offering people ideas, only when they ask us, and only through the language of information and experience, keeps them thinking for themselves. And ironically that language increases the chances that our ideas will penetrate. The language of information and experience is not an interruption. The language of advice is.

So the next time someone asks for your advice, ask them to think about the issue first as far as they can, and if they still want your thinking, give them your ideas in the language of information or experience. Watch them. See if you can spot the lift-off of their thinking. I predict that conforming-to-you will be nowhere. (That is my advice!)

Exclusion

We exclude. We leave people out. Excluding people is a complex thing, in certain ways necessary and so not always wrong, but often. The point here, again, is that as we exclude, we don't see that exclusion as a source of interruption of people's thinking.

In meetings, for example, typically only 30 per cent of the people around the table ever speak (and it is usually the same 30 per cent from meeting to meeting). As they dominate, they exclude. In doing so, they interrupt the thinking, and the potentially valuable contribution, of the excluded. And, ironically, exclusion of the 70 per cent also interrupts the thinking of the 30 per cent because they do not have access to information and perspectives that come only from the silent, excluded ones. Exclusion weakens everyone's thinking.

Identity

Our identities interrupt. They can't help it. They are out there shouting. I think we must face this sure-to-be-upsetting, but undeniable thing: our identities are loaded with judgement – some of it is ours about others', and some of it is others' about ours. If I could do society over, I would delete all identity assumptions from the blueprint. And I would start with the screeching ones: 'I am more' and 'I am less'.

They come in hundreds of shapes and sizes: I am a woman so I am less; I am a man so I am more; I am Black so I am less; I am White so I am more; I am non-binary so I am less; I am cis so I am more; I am Welsh so I am less; I am English so I am more; I am old so I am less; I am young so I am more; I am a clerk so I am less; I am an executive so I am more; I have no legs so I am less; I have two legs so I am more; I am a foreigner so I am less; I was born here so I am more; I am an actor so I am less; I am a producer so I am more; I create hardware so I am less; I create code so I am more . . .

You could settle down for half a day and do nothing but add to that list, skipping lunch. Try listing yours. Then list someone's you don't usually hang out with, or someone's you sit next to at work but wish you didn't.

Then notice this: when someone enters the room, their multiple identities enter first. Apparently, it takes our brains only one sixth of a second to see those identities. So before the person has opened their mouth or even nodded, we have them tidily mored and lessed in our minds. We have to forklift all of that out of the way even to take a step towards the real them. Seeing people as people and not as the assumptions about their identities that society branded into our child brains is exhausting. No wonder we sit down after we say hello.

So it is not a wild leap to see that in the presence of these identity assumptions that stagger their way through our days and fling themselves around our offices and committees and orchestras and governments and schools and families, we cannot think for ourselves. And so we cannot think well together. 'I am more' and 'I am less' annihilate the component of equality. It seems that all identity assumptions are interruptions of our thinking. No question about it: being a decent human being is hard work.

So it is good, and actually invigorating I find, to face the fact that others interrupt our thinking when they, yes, jump on to our sentences, but also when they close their eyes and hurl themselves into our lived moments through advice, exclusion and identity.

And there's more.

Occurrences

The phone rings, the posting pings, the parking expires, the waiter enquires, our baby cries, voices rise, the stomach growls, the north wind howls – things occur. They interrupt us and our attention goes to them, our next thought languishes, or dies. Such is life.

But there are things we can do about this source of interruption. Ahead of time we can turn off the ringer, turn off the pinger, hand over the baby, top up the meter, warn the waiter, find a quiet seat and eat. We can. We are entirely in charge of those occurrences.

As for the 'north wind', we can admire its force and let it become the soundtrack for our thinking session.

Occurrences do not have to be interruption's currency.

Assumptions

But then there are assumptions. The untrue assumptions we live as true. They interrupt our thinking on a regular basis. I didn't use to see untrue assumptions as interruption. But, of course, they are. We can be thinking along, generating insights and possibilities and bold choices; and suddenly, just like that, we're back where we started. We look around. What happened there? Most likely an assumption. An untrue assumption our mind did not, for whatever reason, remove spontaneously while we were thinking. It is an unseen one, usually one we have lived with for a while, safe in the undergrowth of our unexamined life.

I think of an assumption as a kind of pupa. It presages belief. As long as we can catch it and question it, it remains an assumption. But uncaught it will mature into the full creature: a belief. It takes 'rewinding' a belief back to an assumption 'state' in order for it eventually to shrivel completely. In fact, wonderfully, if we just use the word 'assumption' to describe it, that rewinding, shrivelling process begins. Suddenly the belief is an untrue assumption, and seeing its untruth, it withers and we can remove it altogether. That is worth saying again. When we label a belief as an assumption, it becomes one. Words matter.

While we are here, let's pause. Let's look soberly for a moment at 'belief'. Is there a place for 'belief', some people wonder, in a world of independent thinking? Is there a place for creed? Is there a place for unquestioned faith? I've been looking. Hard. I want there to be. But I can't find it.

If a belief is by definition a view that is no longer under discussion, no longer open to scrutiny, a position we agree no longer to question, it cannot live in a world of independent thinking. The minute we decide to think afresh for ourselves about it, it ceases to be a belief.

Therefore, I think we can say that any belief, any creed, tightly held, is an interruption of independent thought.

But maybe, you say, we can hold on to 'beliefs' if we have consciously decided not to question them. If *we decide*. In other words, maybe we are still thinking for ourselves if we *decide* to stop thinking for ourselves.

I'd like that to work. But I don't think it does. You can't be thinking for yourself if you are not thinking for yourself. You may have thought yourself all the way to the decision to stop thinking for yourself, but in stopping you are, well, stopping.

Now that is very different from thinking your way to the conclusion that a belief is true. It then is no longer belief. It is no longer creed. It is fact. But to be fact it has to be provable with logic or information.

Creed is different. It is the regarding as true something that cannot be proven. Creed soon becomes dogma, and dogma punishes divergent, independent thought.

So, no, I don't think belief and fresh independent thinking can coexist. And I think, therefore, that religions, if anchored in obedient adherence to creed, are most likely inherently interruptions of independent thinking, too. It does not mean that religions have no value in our society. But as interrupters of independent thought, they need, I think, our wariness.

So untrue assumptions interrupt us. Uncaught, they can derail us completely and send us back to the never-never land of 'think-for-me' thinking. And there we stay. Stumped, slumping home.

Or not.

Maybe instead someone asks us an 'incisive' question that stands us up straight and lengthens our gait. (We'll see this beauty in action in chapter 40.)

The crucial thing about these four kinds of interruption (ourselves, others, occurrences and assumptions) is that *they are in view.* They are right-here behaviours. We do them and navigate them all day long.

And, yes, they damage. But at least they are there to be seen. We have to become conscious of their impact, but they are visible. And with practice and muscular commitment, we can stop them. We can gradually, one listening minute at a time, eliminate them and free the human mind.

Great, you may say. *I agree. So, once again, shouldn't I just close this book and get out there, promise in hand, and change everything?*

Absolutely.

Actually, just (with apologies to Columbo) one more thing . . .

21. All Around Us: The Interruptive System

You know that world you live in? It's a problem.

And a pretty big one. I know it is not the thing to do these days to call something a problem. It's negative. We should say 'challenge' or 'opportunity' instead. That's fine. But in this case, trust me, it is a *problem*.

In fact, it is *the* one we have to solve. It looks innocent: it's flashy and immediate; it rewards us; it makes us *feel* we are in control. It seems to be nice to us.

But it is a liar. *It* controls *us*. It does this by being an intricate, intentional, invisible, social 'system of interruption'. We have seen how devastating our relationships of interruption are. But social systems of interruption are an even beastlier beast. For one thing, when something is a system, it is potentially a monster. It licks and chews up every single thing it ingests. Our attention, in this case.

The second you close this book and rise from your chair, you are standing inside that system. It is so all around you, it practically *is* you. And its job at this new jump-on-your-steed-and-fight-for-the-promise moment is to run you through.

You might get down the road a teeny bit, persuade a person you know to engage with you in independent thinking by creating a thinking environment with its promise not to interrupt. And you might get a couple of other people to do that, too. Maybe your work teams. Even your family. And all of that will be fabulous. And it will matter. So do it.

But the invisible system of interruption that is the environment of these valiant and valuable steps you want to take can, if not seen for what it is, suck the life out of your resolve, and bring to a crumb-strewn end the thinking relationships you are building.

So before you set out, maybe you would consider this monster 'system of interruption' and look straight at just how we breed it, feed it and inhabit it. Once we see it for what it is, it can no longer shut us up or shut us down. To prevent ravaging by the invisible, we have first to make it visible. Once we do, its power implodes.

As thinking humans wanting thinking relationships in a thinking world, we need to open our eyes.

What we see we can change.

22. Four Systems as One

Systems, by definition, have many pieces. Subsystems, you could say. They need each other. So if we change one piece, we change the whole thing. This system of interruption we're talking about has four main pieces, as I see it, that circle around each other, feed on each other and are eating us alive. (At the risk of seeming gimmicky, I have made up the first two terms. They are accurate, and they'll make sense in a minute.)

They are:

Conformonomics

Digistraction

Persuasion

Polarization

Each is substantive in itself. But again we face the challenge (this time *not* the problem) of talking about a piece when the functioning, the very anatomy even, of that piece depends on the other pieces. But such, as we know, is the nature of language. Unlike music, human language cannot express a whole concept all at once. It has to line up bits and say them one at a time, and just hope for the best. And we have to deal with the frustrating fact that nothing it has just said is completely right because it is only a piece of a piece.

Nevertheless, I'll take each of these four subsystems of interruption in turn, describe it and see if in the end we can hold the bulbous whole.

And then do something about it.

Thankfully.

23. Conformonomics

This system of interruption is huge and gangly and way out of our control (and its own for that matter). It is the multiple parts of our world economy. You may find this exploration exciting. In a furrowed-brow kind of way.

I decided one day to go through the new Oxford mall as a short-cut to the optometrist on Queen Street. For about two years I had watched the mall being built, shuddering at its flatfooted crushing of the ancient, tiny, beloved city of Oxford. But I thought I would take a look.

The underground parking was good, not free, but plentiful.

From the escalator I entered a feast of famous stores. An avenue of 'the best'. Even a Godiva chocolatier, complete now with an espresso bar and cream leather stools.

Unlike other malls, this one was partially open to the sky, not enough for us to get wet should it, because it absolutely would, rain; but just enough to factor a little nature into the fields of tile and glass. I had a perceptible *oomph* in my step as I scanned the choices. I planned. I would buy something for sure. Later.

I walked and walked and walked and walked and walked. I took escalators higher and higher until I could see the spires of Oxford for the first time. I flirted with being excited about that in spite of the alarming incongruence.

I went into this store, that store, the other store, the one just ahead, the one over there, the one with my favourite bath oil, the one with underlit glass shelves holding sheets with a formidable thread count, and one with purses with pockets for every single category of object life could possibly throw up.

I sauntered and stopped and stood and strolled and stopped again. And then, in swells, I started to feel something. Actually, I started to stop feeling anything.

So I sat. I could no longer touch the self that had left home an hour before. I felt weirdly disallowed. My self, my difference, had entered the mall. And then it had disappeared. I had been strolling through repetition. Through derivation. Through deception. The tempters whispered 'choice', but the experience squawked 'conformity'.

I lifted my head and could see that I was sitting in a hall of decisions. Decisions made in far away places by people I would never meet and who more than anything in the world did not want to meet *me*; people figuring out how to produce corridors of conformity so that I would *feel* that I was choosing when all along they had chosen for me.

I could detect the conversations from a few years ago, and still on Monday mornings somewhere in the world, among those few invisible people who are figuring out that if they can own at a distance, if they can buy up the original ideas and products, whip them into a few templates 'appliquéd' to look different from each other, and put them with spotlights and glass into stores all over the world, and then hammer all of those stores together so that as soon as we pop into one, we absolutely will pop into the next and then into the one over there, and back there, not because *we* decide to but because *they* do. The stores are there. They trigger the 'in–out', 'finished/start' spots in our brain. So we enter.

I looked around again. There was nothing original anywhere. Not even the shoppers. They, too, had entered as themselves, and then disappeared coming up the escalator. They carried the same cups and pushed the same ergonomic prams and wore with pride the same expensive holes in their jeans.

Most of all I knew that if I had decided that morning to go to the new mall in Cambridge or in Miami or Hong Kong or São Paulo, or even Paris, I would find the same stores peddling choice while providing none.

I could not think here. Not for myself. That terrified me. So I left. After all, wasn't I just passing through?

I came out on to a little square, walked past a guy's three-table outdoor café, a water colourist's canvas display and a busker singing 'Voi Che Sapete'. I breathed out. Someone smiled at me. I smiled back. That's better. I walked on to Queen Street.

I looked around. Suddenly I stopped feeling again. Chains everywhere. Even the banks, different front doors, different names, different logos. But the same. Even the loans they were making inside, I faced again, have no *selves*. Our mortgage, I found out when we paid it off, was not actually with our bank. It had been dropped into a vat of other loans and stirred into purchases made by a different 'financial institution', and then another. So, where do we bank? I have no idea.

I stood there looking down this ancient street. No one was there. No one with any power or real say or real skin in the game. Sometimes a salesperson smiled, sometimes they were even really good. And occasionally the store manager showed up with a customer-focused hello.

But their somewhere-else bosses and decision-makers had decided before I arrived what my non-choices would be and dressed them in different flavours to build, again, the illusion of choice. This disembodied system was in control of me. I was gone.

I turned away and into the optometrist where I got reasonable expertise and some cute frames, but had to shoo away the same sameness, the chainness, of this place, too. I saved money. But I spent my self. I could not think for myself about anything in there.

I left and walked back to my car, wanting to leave and leave and leave. On my way out I did buy bath gel, and a chocolate, sitting for a moment on the cream leather stool with a hazelnut truffle and a single macchiato. I thought my favourites might help.

They didn't. I was numb for three days. In my heart, in the place where I reside as a one-off, choiceful, independent-thinking human being, I was hard to reach. I had to recover. I did. But I was different. I was starting to see that experience for what it was.

So, Nancy, you might ask me, where have you been? This mall thing, this chain store, absent-owner, entity-invested, choiceless-choice, conformonomics thing has been going on for all of your lifetime and way longer. And you got sick just last week?

86

Exactly. Just last week.

Because I *saw* it.

I had lived it for years. But on that day, I saw it. I saw it for what it is. I saw that it is *interruption*. It is interruption of me as a thinker, a discerner, a chooser, as, in that way, a full human being. I saw it as assault. And I had to wonder: is it a system with no interest whatsoever, ever, ever in what I really think about anything? Nor in what its sellers think about anything? Nor in what anyone at all up the full chain of the chain of chains really thinks?

It's hard not to think so. And if so, this system of our purchasing ho-hum non-choices holds us the way people who interrupt us while we are thinking hold us. Except that when a human being is the interrupter, we can fight back, right there. We can stop the interruption and negotiate a promise between us not to interrupt.

Or at least we can interrupt back. That's not pretty, and it's not effective. But it is something. At least we have a chance of being visible again in a moment. Not very good thinking comes from that volley of interruption, but at the end we both still have our rackets.

This *system* of interruption on the other hand takes the racket away. It interrupts our very autonomy and in turn our collective connection to each other and to the benign authority of true expertise and artistry.

Is it possible, I wonder, that conformonomics has one goal: to make me and all the other visible 'me's out there relinquish our discernment, our delight in true difference, and buy as many of their seen-this-somewhere-before things as possible as fast as possible, so that invisible people somewhere even further afield will buy the system's 'entity/instrument/non-thing' things, so that other unseens can purchase these non-things from them, knowing that they are worthless unless someone else pays even more for them tomorrow? If so, this is a system of interruption of reality itself.

Endless increase and growth are not sustainable, as everyone knows now. They appear also not to be tenable as deliverers of human originality. So is this what we mean by a free market? Isn't this kind of conformity-driven market anything but free?

You are right: I had been purchasing in chain stores and banks for decades. I had assumed that the purpose of the array of chained-together chains was easy access for the customer.

Was it, I now wonder, an on-purpose cocktail of brain hormones to make it hard for the customer to leave? Was it, however solicitously, a planned interruption of independent thinking?

Conformonomics redacts our *selves* from its reports. Sales are up; shareholders are buzzy; we're expanding into five more countries; there will be a few thousand new jobs; we just bought our rival; we will cut a few thousand jobs to keep share value increasing; all is well.

And where are we, the purchasers, the market, the without-whoms the whole thing falls apart? Oh, here we are, following the crumbs into the woods, followed by conformity munching up our way home as fast as it can.

My sister Merl made me laugh when she unwittingly nailed this. I was using a favourite and expensive, all natural of course, designer moisturizer. 'This is so nice,' I said, 'but probably it is the same thing as the drugstore brands.'

'Everything is the same thing,' she said.

Yes . . .

But I am not discouraged. I am confident that independent human minds, freed by the promise of no interruption, by an emerging thinking environment culture, will gradually do new things. Often imperceptibly they will insist on new ways that will result in a produce/sell/buy system fresh and full of colour, driven truly by us and by respect for sustainability, a passion for difference, a disdain for derivation. We can see this already, if we look past the blare and glare of the 'this quarter' obsession that drives decisions.

I also am confident that whole companies, wedded as they seem to be right now to the dictates of conformonomics, are morphing in the direction of systems of no interruption. I draw for my confidence on my times inside the producer end of our purchaser experience. Each time I and others introduce the thinking environment into a giant corporation, we see that executives who make high-level decisions and even higher level salaries are noticing the price they pay for this 'height'. They are seeing that the higher you go, the harder it is to think for yourself, and most certainly to say what you think. They are visionaries. They are impressive exceptions to the organizational system's pervasive injunction to conform. And when their teams 'reconfigure', each of those team members disperses to other positions of influence, sometimes into different companies, and takes the promise of no interruption, of independent thinking, with them.

The more independently we are allowed to think, the more hungry we become for accurate information and logical analysis, for seeing what is right in front of us, and the less prone we are to being scooped up by voices seeking to replace our own.

As I take heart from this long-term effect of independent thinking, I sometimes think about the humans now in utero. I think about how innocently they are developing, how freshly they will enter our world.

And I can imagine that one day new humans will arrive in a world free of our current systems of interruption. They will live in systems of careful and joyful thought, spawned by careful and joyful connection. I can imagine that these new people will naturally nurture those systems, discovering just how rich human life can be, as it tends to all other life.

I can imagine that there will be an occasional bemused but grateful reflection on the fact that just in time, decades ago, people began to think for themselves again, and could see that as humans we are not on the planet, we *are* the planet. And they figured out together how to edge out conformonomics with smarter ways to sustain life. It happened because clear, independent thinking led there. It does, naturally, because it can't not. It is in its nature to nurture.

I cheer a bit now because the thinking environment path to jettisoning sameness is only one path being laid. We live in an era of multiple encroachments on conformity. People are noticing.

Seeing starts it all.

But does all this mean that we shouldn't go to the mall again? No. It means that if we go to the mall, we should go *seeing. Thinking.*

89

Holding on to the self that parked the car. We should see behind the mall to its expression of a systemic, snaking stealthiness of purpose, and not let it sneak into our decisions. We should see the massive system of interruption of self and thinking that it is intended to be. And we should ask ourselves, right now, in this moment, in front of this thing and that thing so like it, and these things we are required to like in order to be liked, what do I really think? What do I really want?

We should go to the mall to practise not being prey.

24. Digistraction

We will have lots of opportunity for this practice because now 'the mall' goes with us. Conformonomics catches a ride with us as we leave. It cooks with us, washes up with us, slouches down into the sofa and sinks into Netflix with us. It even moves with us into formerly sacred sheets. It decides when and how often we wake. It dresses with us, drinks our coffee, goes to our meetings, shops for us, stops by for a beer, races to our child's recital and into our before-bed work catch-up, and into the sheets again. It is the first thing and the last thing we do each day.

It's not that it follows us around. It is that we follow it. We obey this system of designed-in interruption. We live not so much in our houses as on the platforms of the digital world. This translates most of the time to 'on our phones'. They are our location.

Some of us would rather do without our friends than without our phones. That is not a bizarre from-nowhere thing. Like the economic system that feeds on them, digital platforms are *supposed* to interrupt us. And to keep us thrilling when they do, even hoping they will. That is their *purpose*. To keep us theirs.

No, you say, they are designed to connect us. And they do.

Are they? And do they? I'm not so sure. I wonder whether instead they drive us away from the real self, our own and each other's. They interrupt *us*. Because they are supposed to. And I think that in that very act, they stop us from thinking for ourselves.

But what about the good?

Yes, this is, I know, a delicate and complex phenomenon in our lives. It would be easier if this system of interruption, housed in our phones mostly, were all bad. Bad for ourselves and bad for people around us. Like smoking.

But it isn't. It is certainly as addictive. This is well established now. All of the components of addiction are there in digital distraction. If, for example, we 'bottom out' and decide to free ourselves of this addiction, we have to go through the same recovery process we do to stop smoking, drinking, gambling, power-seizing and having out-of-control sex. It's a big deal.

And an even bigger deal, according to James Williams in *Stand Out of Our Light* (one masterpiece you should read immediately), is the hacking of our brains that the injection of ads into our visual field does entirely without our agreement. This colonizing of attentional space is depleting our cognitive autonomy. Our default is no longer to focus. It is to collapse into ads and newsfeeds and profoundly mind-altering distraction.

Yet, so many things about our phones are so good we should cherish them. And I do. I use my phone with thanks for its fast and right-here access to information, and to brief and practical (not sensitive) conversations worth having when we can't call or meet. I adore that my phone takes me fast to the 'library in the sky', as Will Loving, my IT adviser, described the internet in its first year. I like having 'handy' the map apps and the weather forecast and the voice recorder and the notes and FaceTime and, of course, the astonishingly good camera and the near-universe of photo storage. And. And.

I think my phone is also a tiny package of elegance and wonder. To honour that, I amended the line at the bottom of my phone account emails to say, 'Sent from my beautiful iPhone'. I am a little bit in love with its lines and glass. And I wouldn't even consider covering that up with a silicone sleeve. It's pretty, and it's pretty wondrous.

So shall we agree that our phones are all the miracle a person needs, and almost entirely innocent? Then shall we look with eyes and hearts of steel at the other thing? Shall we for this moment face up to the real nature of the thing it hosts: digital interruption? Shall we bear to see that it is not just interruption of our conversations with people, or our concentration at work, or our meetings, or our play with our children, or our lectures or concerts?

Shall we recognize that all of this is severe enough, and documented, but that digital distraction is much more serious even than that? It is a system of interruption of us as independent thinkers. And not just because it interrupts our thinking. But because its immersing of us in conformity for hours each day slowly blunts our interest in, possibly even our elegant capacity for, thinking beyond the givens to our very own perceptions and thought.

And shall we face the fact it is intended to do exactly that? Only if we slowly deskill ourselves by living in this invisible chamber of conformity every day do we become sufficiently groomed to obey the come-this-way features of conformonomics. That is the point to take home. The distraction capability is built into the very architecture of the social platforms our phones host and that we love. This interruption of us as independent thinkers seeps through its vents. And in no time, as thinkers we stop breathing.

That is why I think of it as *digistraction*. It is a single thing. And it is intended to be.

To start, it is tempting to think of this interruption of thinking as manifesting just in the pings and vibrations of push notifications for texts, emails and postings. But those pings really aren't the problem. I know they are pervasive. There is even something called 'phantom notifications', imagined pings, that people report more and more often to their therapists. So I am not minimizing the impact of the pings on our ever-eroding attention.

But those interruptive acts are completely within our control. We just have to 'deselect' them. We usually don't. Addiction is like that. We *can* quit, but we don't. But in understanding distraction as a system of interruption of our independent thinking, it is crucial to know that we can turn them off.

The bigger dimension of digistraction is in the platform itself. This feature we cannot turn off. You sign on for one thing, but to get it, you have to get another thing as well. It would be like asking for water but having to get ricin, too.

This is the digital ricin: a multi-image page with a changing peripheral field, jerking our attention from ads to friends' posts, to newsfeeds, to videos. These platforms do not allow us on unless we first agree to be distracted. We cannot select for a clean, radiant, single-focus page. We cannot choose no ads. We can click the X in the almost-invisible box in the right-hand corner sometimes. But it immediately asks us why we did that. And in no time it is back with a different ad. On these platforms we cannot deselect distraction.

And even this architecture of distraction is not the molten centre of the problem we are facing. That core is the fact that multiple distractions chemically kill discernment. Distractions, as we have seen, raise anxiety, i.e. cortisol and adrenaline, in the brain. These hormones in turn reduce our ability to think for ourselves. They make us want to give in to the wandering hands of distractors. This design of distraction is, therefore, not an oh-I-apologize, just-ignore-me-please by-product of the platform architecture. It is the goal of the architecture. It sets out to *generate the hormones that make us want* more distraction.

Just as one drink of alcohol chemically makes us *want* another drink, one distraction produces dopamine and oxytocin in the brain, *making us want* another distraction. And another. Until we fall over and can't remember the next morning quite what happened. We can see that we made some bad decisions during the binge, and our relationships need a few repairs, and somehow we banged the car in it all, but otherwise everything seems good, and everyone is drinking again today, so I'll have one, too. Now. Before I shower.

It is a physical thing.

We do hear about this, of course. We read about it. Maybe we even discuss it in groups or on a leadership training course, or in couples counselling because of the affairs we are having with our phones. But we cannot bear truly to see it. If we do, we will have to give up the menacing but mesmerizing immediacy of pseudo control, the made-up, mainlining pleasure of it.

So what can we do?

First, we can face all of this. We can stop pretending. We can admit to ourselves that if we are scrolling and tapping and clicking, and the person with us is talking, we are not listening. We're not. So we can stop saying we are. We may be hearing enough not to reply so stupidly we might as well have left the room. But this is not listening. This is not respect. And it is not generative of good thinking.

We also can stop saying things like 'I grew up distracted so I am not actually distracted. I have adapted.' Or 'What really distracts me is the anxiety I feel when my phone is off.' Or 'My friends and I feel truly connected when we are posting and checking and sharing. We can't really connect without our phones.' Or 'If we both are on our phones, it works for our relationship; we are differently connected in that way. Nothing bad is happening to our marriage or our family.' Or 'It takes too much time to talk.'

He's not drunk. He just likes sleeping on the floor.

So first we can tell our phones not to alert us. And we can decide to check only when alone and only then about as often as we eat (unless you are a committed grazer). Something like that. You will find your own way to an in-charge, undistracted relationship with the notification system on your phone. You can. That's what matters.

The other thing, though, the root, is harder. It is very like the system of conformonomics, and the other two systems of interruption coming up. Digistraction permeates and is the platform itself. We can't undo this distraction architecture.

But as with conformonomics, we can see it for exactly what it is. And we can decide just how much of our ability to think for ourselves we want to hand over to those particular attention-pilfering forces we carry in our hands. We can populate the platforms the way we might walk the post-war battlefields, gingerly, cognizant of the blasting apart of brilliance that lurks beneath.

To become the one in charge of my digital life, I have now turned off all notifications (and that was not exactly easy; they really don't want you to do that). I now have to *decide* to look. If I raise the phone, only the time comes up. No texts. I also keep my phone out of sight most of the time and mostly out of reach. I won't even have dinner with anyone who has to have their phone on the table, even if it is off. I also won't attend family gatherings unless everyone agrees that almost all of our time together will be with no phones visible or audible.

Every meeting I chair and every group I teach is an interruption-free zone, and that means digital devices inaudible, invisible. If we need the internet, we use it on purpose and with discipline.

I moved gradually to this action. I had watched the connections among my delegates and their connection to their learning dissolve as soon as the breaks began and the phones came out. After a few years I had become unwilling to foster this loss any more. And I realized I was willing to lose business if necessary in order to stop this infiltration of the platform system of interruption. I wanted to restore the full, attentive, undistracted human mind to every minute of our study and practice. I have lost no business.

I now ask that people manage their lives before they come so that they can be undisturbable all day. And if they absolutely, as in someone might be dying, have to check their phones, could they please do it away from the view and hearing of the rest of us.

I am difficult.

But people tell me they are grateful. They will pay, they say, for the requirement to be present. They say there is a longing in them. I understand that. The human mind does, I think, want to return and do its beautiful work for itself again. It is listening for the relief helicopters in the distance.

So I persist.

All of this evolved. It started on a walk with a friend at least a decade ago. Suddenly where there had always been just the two of us, there was a phone. Between us. Uninvited. Unagreed. Emergency? Well, no, just checking. Sorry.

Then it was the three of us always. Just in case. Of? I know. But the sound's off.

Then, here's a photo, and another, oh and this one. And these. And just a second, I'll post that one. Hey, Jean got the job!

My friend was 'just checking' us away from each other.

Soon I gave in and brought mine, too, and when she checked, I checked. But I was sad. I knew what real connection was between us, and this was not it.

Slowly it seemed as if most of the people in my life were only occasionally here. Even the nice strangers on the street were gone. Good morning? Nope. Sometimes they bumped into me, or they swerved just in time. So sorry.

During this period I decided to despair privately. Apparently, no one but me was concerned about this, and my growing alarm was saturated with sadness, and so seemed unobjectively, untrustworthily personal.

Then I came across Linda Stone, Microsoft executive and writer. Her famous concept of 'continuous partial attention' helped me. Her view came from research, not from personal 'bereavement', so I felt I could trust it. And I could finally see why I was so unsettled by my tense or disappearing friends. She said:

> Continuous partial attention is an always on, anywhere, anytime, any place behaviour that creates an artificial sense of crisis. We are always in high alert. We are demanding multiple cognitively complex actions from ourselves. We are reaching to keep a top priority in focus, while, at the same time, scanning the periphery to see if we are missing other opportunities. If we are, our very fickle attention shifts focus.
>
> The latest, greatest powerful technologies are now contributing to our feeling increasingly powerless.

She helped me see the root of my despair: with the thinking environment I was teaching *continuous full* attention to produce *fully independent* thinking; whereas the phone was inculcating *continuous fragmented* attention, producing *fully dependent* thinking because the platform system's revenue depends on it. I was teaching deep connection. Platforms were teaching superficial connection. I was teaching attention. Platforms were teaching interruption.

So my despondency I could now understand. And maybe forgive. That helped. Understanding usually does.

But Stone was a lone voice for me for a few years. I was beginning to despair out loud. Others were agreeing with me, and we were commiserating. But I was disconsolate.

Then my inbox began to fill up with research about this thinking-reduction feature of digital distraction, compelling publications from multiple fields of knowledge, including an almost unbelievable study finding that when people's phones are visible, even if they are off and everyone knows they are, 'The mere presence of their smartphone was enough to reduce their cognitive capacity' (Assistant Professor Adrian Ward, McCombs School of Business, University of Texas, Austin).

Fifty studies later, I am more and more concerned, but selfishly relieved that it is not just the whitespace-loving, ease-championing, attention-enamoured me that is the problem.

In fact, just the other day I was sent an analysis of this phenomenon by Alan Lightman, physicist and writer:

By not giving ourselves the minutes – or hours – free of devices and distractions, we risk losing our ability to know who we are and what's important to us. The destruction of our inner selves via the wired world is a subtle phenomenon. The loss of slowness, of time for reflection and contemplation, of privacy and solitude, of silence, of the ability to sit quietly in a chair for fifteen minutes without external stimulation – all have happened quickly and almost invisibly.

The situation is dire. We are losing our ability to know who we are and what is important to us. We are creating a global machine in which each of us is a mindless and reflexive cog, relentlessly driven by the speed, noise, and artificial urgency of the wired world.

I would like to make a bold proposal: that half our waking minds be designated and saved for quiet reflection.

We need a mental attitude that protects stillness, privacy, solitude, slowness, personal reflection; that honors the inner self; that allows each of us to wander about without schedule within our own minds.

Yes.

But then my car gave in to its age. I decided to buy a new one. That was not in itself upsetting. And it all went smoothly. But there was one moment that was so disturbing I had to drive away and think about it.

This was the problem. Every new car has – I know you know this – a dashboard video screen. So even while we are driving and risking lives, digistraction grabs us. One day this will be illegal. At least when a car's Bluetooth system was just for audio, we had to decide to pick up the phone if we wanted to see messages and to do the illegal and pathological thing of reading and replying while driving.

But now the car itself has become our phone. It has made the decision to be 'on' so easy it seems ultra retro not to use it. And as with the phone itself, the touchscreen produces in us a *feeling* of control by keeping us craving *its* control, clicking its yes/no choices even when we are driving, hurling us out of attention and into distraction and, thereby, into danger. Threatening lives. Everyone's.

And just in case you haven't kept up with the research on dangerous driving, talking, even hands-free, on the phone in a car is the danger equivalent of driving under the influence of alcohol. So if you are the 'designated driver' but you are on the phone in your car, you might as well be drunk.

Heaven knows what the equivalent is to hearing your texts and telling Siri what to say in reply, checking your posts and even just moving from the FM icon to the iPhone icon and its addictive this/ that choice. Basically, I figure that if the manoeuvre takes our eyes off the road, it is a killer. We should not do it.

Will it take the child we kill who darted out from between two cars while we were tapping our screen or talking to Siri before we actually *see* this system of interruption? This interruption of us as thinkers?

The next day I asked if I could deselect for screen viewing. No. After you get in and start the engine, you can tap a button once and then twice and darken the screen. *But* first you are required to see its two-only choices: iPhone or radio, map or fuel? Siri or not? First you have to navigate the distractions. But of course, then you can choose none of them and darken the screens. Sure.

Oh, except for one thing. Even if you have tapped twice for dark, the minute you shift into reverse, the screen comes on again. And there before you is a make-believe image of your path behind. You are expected to surrender your direct sense of the path and the objects around your car for someone else's idea of them who is not even there and who figured out what 'close' is in a design room somewhere about two years ago. I know a woman who says that this feature is saving her life. She truly does not know what she would do now if that back-up picture feature were not there. This is a woman who has been backing up without that feature for more than forty years. And she never killed herself doing it. Not once.

This secondary sensing phenomenon is actually erosive. Matthew Crawford, in his *The World Beyond Your Head* (another masterpiece you should read before you do a single other thing), says that one of the ways we lose our ability to think is to surrender it to secondary sensing devices. We stop thinking when we obey the perceiver that is not in the room. When we allow a *picture* of our reality to replace our felt/touched/heard/seen reality, we take a step away from, again, our real selves. And our brains anaesthetize a bit of their capacity to judge where we are in the physical world.

And no, this feature cannot be disabled.

I bought the car. I love it for everything else. And its screen is smaller than some. I decided to feel good about that. Besides, I darken it almost always. But I have to summon lashings of self-regulation to make that choice. The built-in, get-distracted, I'm-going-to-interrupt-you-immediately feature of that screen is expected to be adored by the new consumer. The designers think we want to be pushed into distraction as soon as we push the key-less ignition. They've roamed the nobody-streets, too.

I wonder if they would sell fewer cars if the screen started as dark and stayed dark until – *until* – the driver clicked three things to turn it on, and then had to confirm that choice? Um, nice car, really like it. But I think I'll go down the road to the other place where I can buy an immediate way to be distracted, and thus feel in control while not being.

Selling cars, selling anything, is the act of raising emotion and self-esteem, as we all have known for ages. So, we would say these days that we are way ahead of the ads that used, for example, the female almost-naked form to make us identify as sexy and to make our cars identify as an experience of carnal pleasure. We see right through that now. Aren't we good?

But we don't see its current version: 'I am important because I get to feel in control by looking and tapping and talking to an algorithm.' At least before when we got in, we could tell that the car was not a female body. Today we actually think the car is an experience of choice. We cannot tell that we are not free; we are fodder.

How far can this go?

Cars are the least of it. Even the expressly let's-be-together places like restaurants, including posh ones, are becoming creepy meeting points where people arrive together, then sit 'apart'. Recently a party of six arrived at their table. And every single one of them, before they looked at each other, pulled out their phones and touched their screens to bring forth hundreds of other people who were not invited, some of whom they had never met.

That act in itself was a desecration of the culinary artist's design and preparation of the place for them, and it was thus disturbing to any aesthetic still breathing in the room. But the creepy part was how uncreepy that act was to them. Intentional, and now normalized, disconnection and desecration? That's pretty creepy if you ask me.

The most serious platform crisis, though, is in our closest relationships. The real loss is of the people we treasure.

A friend asked me what he could do to restore his family. 'No one has any attention for anyone else any more. Everyone is checking their phones, responding, and checking again. Everyone is with someone else all of the time. Janey even brings hers to bed.'

A young colleague told me he hankers way too often for the time when he and his wife were dating. 'We listened to each other then. But mainly we weren't on our phones. Sure, we pulled them out to share a picture or two, or a saved message from a mutual friend. But then we put them away.

'We don't do that now. They are on the kitchen table and the dinner table and the bedside table, and in our hands as we walk out the door and walk back in at the end of the day. We just are not together any more. Not together together. I wonder if we even would know what to say or how to draw each other out any more if we weren't being interrupted.'

I think most of us fall in love mainly because the person listened to us. Not impeccably most likely, but better than anyone else ever had. And the first deep change that happens as the relationship matures is not cessation of sex but cessation of listening. Our attention for each other erodes. We blame it on the demands that come home with us from work, and the work demands at home. We blame it on the needs of children. Those are all real challenges, of course. But the actual problem is the shifting of dating culture, which is a culture of listening, to a marriage culture, which is a culture of interruption.

Some people try to repair that tear by having 'date nights'. This is laudable. But they tell me that it helps only a tiny bit because the phones are on the table. And soon just below the thumb.

I predict that fairly soon the courts will recognize 'neglect by digistraction' as grounds for divorce. There will probably even be country songwriters going gold with metaphors for 'the other woman' not as whisky, but as phones.

I am confident that there will one day be a movement from young people themselves to keep phones out of friend time and group time, out of learning time and time with family and beloveds. It will be its own kind of revolution, led by the very people who, because they were born into it, were supposedly immune.

So I am beginning to understand what is unscrupulous about the car screens, why some restaurants now are forbidding phones, why some families now have phone-free meals and evenings, why some couples keep the phone not only out of the bedroom, but out of reach except by agreement, why some business executives take phones away from anyone who uses them during a meeting and put them into buckets of water. There is a lot of salvaging starting up.

And I understand where everyone has gone. I understand why these nowhere people are everywhere.

Both Williams and Crawford see this crisis of attention as a crisis of self-regulation.

No, you say. I disagree about the age thing. I think it is different with the grew-up-with-it generation. It just is. It's almost in their genes.

As we have seen, this argument is still out there even though it has been discredited. Lore lingers. So it really doesn't become us to assert this hopeless defence of platform addiction.

Instead we need to face the fact that designed-in interruption of thinking and of self does not care about, nor depend on, what age its victims are or how early in their lives they took to the digital world. Or how 'fluent' they are in it. It works because it works. It was designed to get human beings of every age to click 'to extinction'. It is acceptable to whomever; and it is upsetting to whomever. Being born into the decades of digital dominance does not make people immune to its brain-co-opting intentional designs. It is not somehow different and healthful for people, just because they are children whose first toys were swipe and click objects, to engage in disengagement as a way of life.

Their very comfort with it is, if anything, the thing to worry about. As we know, the younger the prey, the more dangerous the predator. 'Give me a child until he is seven . . .'

But I am not hopeless about this either.

Yesterday I was in a café, writing some of this book. To my left a family of three sat down. They ordered breakfast. The daughter was about seven. She said how fun this was. Her mother agreed. And her father. A treat on a weekday. The daughter giggled: she wanted extra jam on her pancakes. The father pretended a frown. They laughed. I smiled into my cup.

Then both parents pulled out their phones. Tap, scroll, swipe. Eyes, thoughts, attention? All gone. The daughter, cell by cell, hunched. She sucked the straw of her juice glass, looking over it to her mother and across it to her dad and down again. The fun? All gone. The mother looked up. She set her phone down. The daughter leaned in, caught her eyes. Then lost them. Her mother swiped again. The food came. A split moment of smiles. Then swipes. They left, the daughter looking all the way up the long adult for perchance a glance.

Another family of three entered and sat down at the table across from me. The daughter and son, probably eight and ten, sat opposite their mother. They bounced into their seats, wiggled their feet and smiled at each other. The mother opened her purse. My heart sank.

But out of her purse came two decks of cards. She dealt them. They played. They laughed; they gasped; they smiled; they studied each other; they conspired; they celebrated; they analysed. They finished. And she dealt again. Breakfast came. They ate and giggled some more.

As they were gathering their things to leave, I got up and moved to the chair next to their table. 'I want to thank you,' I said. 'I am writing a book about developing human intelligence and about the power of sustained engagement with each other as a culture for independent thinking. As far as I am concerned, you are at the cutting edge of this as a family. No actual or digital interruption of your connection with each other at all. Only consistent contact the whole time. I admire you.'

She did not throw her arms around me or even say how lovely of me to notice. She probably wondered how this American busybody had been allowed in. But she did smile. And she said a soft thank you. And I smiled back. Her daughter did, too.

Maybe I won't do that next time. Maybe I'll just stay at my table and be pleased in private.

But if there is a next time, I will note that it was not the first time. I will hope that it was another bump. And that there will be another. I have been in a real earthquake, and I know how fast they can develop once they get going. And how thoroughly the structures fall that ignored the geology in their construction.

The human mind needs structures of attention and connection. If instead it gets structures of interruption, of distraction, it will, I have faith, eventually move its plates and collapse them. And contrary to our current lore about the young, it will be the young that move the plates.

All this, while – as with the system of conformonomics – the millennials and middle-agers in power submit themselves to withering fragmentation. They comply with the salary-paying forces that have designed these systems of churned-out work and market deceptions.

All workers (especially executive workers, as we have noted) have to be prevented from thinking for themselves because they might pop up with that inconvenient question: 'Tell me again, why are we doing it this way?' That would slow everything down. So these potential thinkers have to be all day long in environments of obedience. Obedient environments are by nature environments of distraction and interruption. And what could be a better re-enforcer of that think-like-us system than the listen-to-me-not-to-each-other chortling Charybdis of the digital platform?

How far can this go?

Too far. Conformonomics and digistraction love each other.

For example, I think of myself as unshockable. But recently I was asked to lecture at a famous business school. I agreed. I absolutely assumed that they would be up on the research about the cognitive-slowing effects of phone presence in groups. I arrived. I had coffee with one of the professors. He would introduce me, and we were to go over what he would say. I told him the main points of my usual introductory material and then said perfunctorily that I would appreciate his also confirming the digital-distraction-free norm.

His face seemed to compress. I quickly added that my segment did not require access to the internet and that phone distraction was an interruption of independent thinking.

He said that actually they didn't have a digital-distraction-free norm. They just wouldn't be able to get clients if they did. We do, he said, encourage people not to look at their phones any more than necessary. And he agreed to make a special point of it today because of the unusual subject of my presentation. I thanked him, though in my head I shook my head, and headed down the hall.

The students arrived. Phones came out. The professor made the request. People scowled. Some sighed. Some silenced their devices and put them away. Some didn't.

What disturbed me most in that moment was that this freedom from digital interruption was an exception to their norm. Their norm is interruption. And so there emerged a posture of resentment undulating from table to table. I had to decide from minute to minute how much of an authoritarian deal to make of it.

I tried to comfort myself, the way you do when you have a

blowout on the motorway and are just grateful it was not a jack-knifed lorry in front of you, that here at least, unlike the faculty of another prestigious business school, this professor was not remind-ing the students of the school's hashtag so that they could tweet during my lecture. But that heroic act of perspective didn't work. I was off-centre in my centre. The defiance in the room, the addic-tion splayed across the tables and soon the active 'checking and replying' distracted me and others. I could not 'hold' the group as I like to because I could not think at the edge; and neither could they.

Most people said the presentation was good and the client asked for it again. I agreed as long as from the beginning of the course, weeks before I arrived, the professor would strengthen the school's request for no phone distraction by explaining that intelligence is lowered when the phones are discernible.

But to do that I had to weigh what the students do internalize about the promise of no interruption and the components of a thinking environment against what they don't internalize about addiction to distraction. Life is never linear, so I continued to pre-sent, to explain the digital-free request and to focus on the majority who are willing to be for three hours unshackled to their phones.

For all of the hours on either side of my segment, though, they are absorbing only a portion of what is being taught and experi-enced because a part of their brain is always with the potential or actual interruption by the phone and by the system of interruption that imbues their beings now. So these leadership students are learning to lead by distraction.

And even more subtly but powerfully, they are becoming slightly more stupid rather than smarter from their experience of the course. They are continuing to re-enforce the reduction of cognitive hor-mones in the brain, the lowering of their functional intelligence, that distraction causes. The soul-saddening irony is that it should be exactly in centres of learning that intelligence increases.

But we have choice.

We can keep eroding our relationships and weakening our think-ing. Or we can do something about this. We can pay loads to be unplugged at a digital-free resort. We can download an app that paces our phone use. Or we can think about how much our very best self wants to commit each day to the thought-stripping, reactive state of digistraction.

We can notice digistraction, like conformonomics, as a polluter of thinking. First, we can face it for real, as in I-knew-it-was-bad-but-god.

And we can dignify our autonomous, in-charge selves and live our lives according to the impact they are having, not on the lust they are feeding.

We are dazzling. We can act like it. It feels good once we get going. We just need to start.

So how much can you focus, how much more present can you be today, how much longer can you listen, how much further can you think before you check and scroll? How much can you see before you look? How much can you love before you leave?

Conformonomics and digistraction are predators.

And they are not alone.

25. Persuasion

There is a third one. You'll need your boots for this. It makes the sinister systems of conformonomics and digistraction seem very Norman Rockwell. It is fiendishly complex and counter-intuitively predates the economic systems and technology that drive the first two. It is human-species old.

So, it is almost impossible to see. We can be forgiven for being its hapless target most of our lives. We can be forgiven for becoming in a matter of minutes the panting, gawking, wilfully blind hem-kissers of self-appointed saviours. We can be forgiven for not seeing them in front of our star-spinning eyes, and for laying our brains at their altar. And thus we can be forgiven for not thinking for ourselves around them.

Nevertheless, being in thrall is no way to be in charge. To the extent that we need someone to be right so that we can keep adoring them, we abandon our capacity to see, and thus our capacity to think for ourselves. History is full of the social devastation that such abandonment produces.

Actually, this everywhere thinking-suppressing system is not the playground of only the sociopaths of the world. We all do it to a degree. Gandhi and Martin Luther King did it. You do some of it, too. So do I. I am doing some of it here. It is what works to get people to consider us. A bit like Machiavellian thought, often confused with prescriptions for evil, persuasion is merely pragmatism. It is what works. It is amoral. But if we are ignorant of it, it can stop us from thinking for ourselves. So we need to understand it in order to notice it when it is underway.

And to do that, as with all systems of interruption in which we do our breathing and our thinking (or not), we have to see it. So here it is.

Persuasion can appear in multiple forms. Do one, you get

people's attention. Do five, you have people by the throat. Do all on a regular basis, and people are yours forever. They will become willing to overlook, justify or interpret as good everything bad you do.

I first began to understand this system of persuasion through the research and writing of Professor Charles Cialdini (*Influence: the Psychology of Persuasion*) and Scott Adams (*Win Bigly*) whose books have become for me two more don't-leave-the-house-before-you-read-it musts.

Drawing on their observations and on ours over the years, I offer here twelve ways to persuade people, to get them thinking like, and liking, you. In a moment I'll suggest how they act as systems of interruption and keep us from thinking for ourselves.

1) First Context
Be *first* in framing an issue, particularly in the media, so that it and you become the context for the discussion, the reference point for everyone else's take, requiring your detractors to respond to *you* rather than be heard freshly first for their own points. In that way, stay the focus.

2) Attention Control
Change what people pay attention to. Regardless of other important issues in their life, direct their attention to you, particularly to you as the answer to their problems. People regard as important anything that has their attention.

3) Identity
Speak to the way people *see themselves*, making them see you as *one of them*. Become 'their voice'. Do this in two ways:

- Say explicitly the improper, 'politically incorrect' things people are thinking but are hesitant to say out loud because 'people like us don't say those things'. Make the unsayable sayable.

- 'Dog whistle'. Produce 'cognitive dissonance' by alluding to, but not saying explicitly, things people think unconsciously but won't admit to themselves because 'that is not who we really are'. Make the unthinkable thinkable.

4) 'Kill Shots'
Label people. Label your detractor with a derisive word or phrase that is unusual in the context. Label yourself and your followers with a positive word.

5) Repetition
Say multiple times in a row the things you want people to remember, especially the 'kill shots'. People begin to regard as true the things they hear over and over.

6) Unpredictability
Act in unpredictable, unorthodox ways, keeping people off balance and thus gripped, wanting to tune in to you whenever they can.

7) Stories
Use narrative and imagery. Avoid data and concepts.

8) Brevity
Keep key points, stories, sentences, and even words, short.

9) Reassigning Trust
Cast aspersions on formerly trusted authorities if they oppose you. Cast yourself as the one trustworthy authority.

10) Talking Past the 'Sale'
Draw a verbal picture of the future people want, as if that future were now.

11) Praise
Start with a positive comment about the person or group you want to persuade.

12) **Preparation for Martyrdom**

Claim victory, regardless of the factual outcome. Characterize any defeat as the ignorance and selfishness of your detractors, not as your failure. In that way sustain allegiance, even past your death.

Fine. Fascinating. Important.

But scary.

Yes.

And no.

We do need to accept that the power of persuasion at its worst lies in its *design to interrupt*. It is supposed to interrupt *us*, our independent, cogent, thinking selves. And it does.

And of course it is true that unlike the systems of conformonomics and digistraction, persuasion is inescapable. Human relationships are inherently engagements with persuasion. It is the nature of humans to seek to persuade. And we do all day long, every day, through conversation with each other, through books, ads, art, media, marches, preachers, rituals. Everything. Wherever humans show up, we attempt to persuade. And so we are at this systemic level interrupting each other's independent thinking much of the time. (This is one reason why our conscious decisions to generate independent thinking in ourselves and others is so vital.)

Adams and Cialdini say that these behaviours of persuasion will capture us even if we know about them. I agree and disagree. They do for sure entice us. They can get us into the persuader's orbit and even into their personal aura.

But in my experience, once there, if we know what they are doing and can see it start up, we are free to decide for ourselves whether to resist or to stay. When we don't know about this persuasion system, we are not free to choose. We just stay. We stop thinking for ourselves. Recognizing the system at work, on the other hand, we stay intact as thinkers.

Persuasion happens everywhere. Recently I noticed that a salesperson was employing five of the persuasion forms. So I said, 'Hi, I know what you are doing. And you are good at these persuasion techniques. They are working. I want your product. I can picture myself pleased with this. So you can stop doing them now.' He chuckled. And he started talking facts and figures. We were both happy.

But the next day a vendor said as I walked by in the Friday market, 'Hi there. What a lovely shirt you're wearing. Brightens my day.' I recognized his persuasion tactics, stopped, looked at his product, determined I did not want to learn about it and said, 'I know what you are doing. I'm afraid it is not working.' I smiled. 'Thanks anyway.' He smiled back. I walked on.

I walked on as a whole and independent thinking person, having, yes, to bat away the interruptive system of persuasion, but not as its ignorant casualty.

Being persuaded or not to buy something is one thing. And, of course, it matters. People spend a lot of time 'in the market'. But being persuaded to *think* something matters more. Ideas can stay with us for a lifetime. And some of them can affect the whole world. Politics is the most obvious peddler of ideas, a veritable orgy of persuasion. And each of us is actively vulnerable inside it. So it is doubly a good thing if we can see the persuasion system at work there and defy its interruption of our own thinking.

This political arena of persuasion has worked both ways in me. One candidate immediately corralled my allegiance. His picture of the future I long for ('talking past the sale'), his speaking to the real nature of who we are as human beings ('identity'), his repetition of phrases that perfectly captured the changes he would make ('repetition'), his saying things I thought were too bold and anti-mainstream for people like us to say ('cognitive dissonance') and his narratives that captured my own experience uncannily ('stories') had me from the first speech. I wanted the ride to last unimpeded forever. I was sold.

But like saying no to guacamole (93 per cent impossible for me), I peeled my enthusiasm away from my heart and stepped back. I could see what was happening. The system of persuasion had interrupted me. I was thinking like him. I was nowhere. I took a few breaths, said goodbye to the bliss of believing and asked myself,

'What do I – *I* – think here? If he had been old, glued to a script, long-winded, told zero stories, dumped data everywhere and said everything only once, would I sign up? And if I knew that I can think at least as well as he can, what would I do (and feel) here?'

That little retrieval of my drowning self was a big job, but it felt good after I dried off. And I did start to think for myself about him, about his ideas, about his character, about the plausibility of his reasoning and the relative likelihood of his being able to do one single thing he said he would do if elected.

I signed up. But as myself. Not as him.

Another time, the opposite happened. The man repelled me from the first minute. He used all twelve persuasion tactics in one speech, but they didn't work. His values were a million miles from mine. I saw him as the dark side of persuasion. I was proud not to be hooked.

And then I realized I was. I was hooked *against* him. And it was just as big a job to step back from my repulsion now as it had been from my adoration before. I did not want to come to my senses and actually think about what he was saying. I needed him to be entirely wrong because he was entirely reprehensible. But I breathed twice, as before, and staggered away from the perverse pleasure of hating him. I began to think about the things he had said. Out of eighty, I agreed with three. I half agreed with two others. I let myself look at the whole package, from a distance.

I wholeheartedly did not sign up. But I was thinking, not retching. And it was good to know that there was nothing he could do to take my mind away. Unthinking rejection is the same thing as unthinking embrace. In both cases we are gone.

An important note here: at some point along the way we always pay as positive persuasion pawns. Allowing our own thinking and clear feeling to be interrupted by persuasion will, in the end, end us. My colleague learned this sharply when she put all her influence, time and enthusiasm behind a candidate. He owed his votes largely to her. He won. And then he betrayed her. She was shocked.

Then she began to learn about the annihilating force of persuasion and soon, sober, was shocked at having been shocked. Seeing is like that. We simply cannot fathom that we had not seen what was right there. I call it 'disappointment in allegiance'. It takes a lot of recovering from. It is a direct result of handing over our thinking to someone else because we did not climb out of the system of persuasion in time – because we did not know we were in it.

What pulls us in so far so fast? The identity tactic (number 3 above). And how? By making us think they and we are one. If the persuader makes us feel that they are one of us, however outrageously different they are from us, they have us. A common version of this usurpation of identity is the persuader's declaration: 'I will be your voice.' They will speak for us. They will *think* for us. They will become our real and formerly unexpressed selves.

This is alarming on many levels. Most dangerous is that we soon cannot allow them to be wrong, regardless of what they do or say. If they are wrong, our own beings become wrong. *We* are at stake in what they do or say. And so we can no longer hear them or face them squarely. We hear and see only the *us* in them. We must protect them because we must protect ourselves. Trace the allegiance levels of persuaders who have said, 'I will be your voice'. It isn't pretty.

Again, what can we do?

Well, they don't say 'knowledge is power' for nothing. And now you have it. So try it. Now that you know what persuasion, whatever its motive, consciously or not, is up to, notice. Then 'step back' and think. Do you actually embrace this product, this idea, this job, this policy, this date? If you knew that you are terrific no matter what this person thinks of you, that what you really think is at least as worthy as whatever they want you to think, that you are completely good and that saying no to them can be a statement of integrity, not an insult, what would you do now? What do you really think?

That set of questions changes the zone – from theirs to yours. You are no longer captive. You are you. *You* decide.

Knowledgeable of these systems of interruption, we can see not only each one but also the ways they spawn, suckle and exacerbate the other two. The numbing non-choice of the conformonomics system hooks the pseudo control of the distraction system, and it fertilizes the system of persuasion to finish the job. All three interruptive systems are systems of disconnection: separating us from ourselves and from other people.

It is grim at one level, but equipped with 'recognition gear', we step clear of it, staying in charge of our own minds. And because we do, because we stand knowledgeable of the conformonomics, digistraction and persuasion systems around us, we become their observer, not their kill. Those interruptive systems no longer hijack us. They are just part of the 'information' dimension of our environment. So we can think.

Extrication from those three systems of interruption – there is nothing quite like it . . .

26. Polarization

. . . except for the fourth. Extrication from it is sheer heroism – probably because this system is the one that destroys specifically our ability to think *together*. It interrupts us all.

Polarization snaps our thinking necks in two. Cerberus-like, it is a system of interruption, a cause of it and its result, all at once. And like the other three systems of interruption, it becomes how we live until we understand how it works. So as before, we first have to *see* it.

To begin, consider afresh that polarization is a phenomenon not of disagreement, but of disconnection. I can disagree with you even about things sacred to us both, but our disagreements do not polarize us. It is when we disconnect from each other as human beings that we polarize. Once we disconnect and polarization begins (when we suddenly judge the other to be irretrievably wrong and ourselves to be unassailably right), we disconnect further, and we polarize more.

And more. Soon we cannot speak to each other. Sometimes we give up on each other completely.

Some have called polarization 'the new war'. Others have called it 'the other climate change'. They both capture its catastrophic potential.

And it's funny because, of the four systems of interruption, polarization is probably the most painful and complex. Yet it is also the easiest to stop. Unlike the other three, it is not everywhere. It is a dramatic, externally occurring change. We notice it. It hurts. We hate it. As it takes us over, we acknowledge it.

All four systems *cause* interruption. But polarization is also directly *caused by* it. And so to stop it, we have simply (although, of course, not easily) to eliminate the cause: we agree not to interrupt.

If we can do that, we will not polarize. We will disagree. Even deeply. We may fight. Even fiercely. But we will not disconnect. And if we don't disconnect, we will keep thinking.

Really?

You may be shaking your head at my naivety. Surely it is not that simple. Not this. Not this behemoth that is polarization.

It is a behemoth, I agree. But so is interruption. And as for 'not that simple', Oliver Johnston, one of the finest thinkers I know, said that 'the thinking environment holds the kind of simplicity that is to be found on the far side of complexity'. Interruption heaves with complexity, with everything needed to cause personal and societal disconnection.

Also, our polarized responses have all the fingerprints of interruption: we recoil; adrenaline and cortisol race like wild things around our brains; we sweat; we stop breathing; we respond with fear as the life-endangered creatures we feel we are in that moment. Clearly, interruption, or something very like it, has just happened.

Plus, consider this: when we interrupt in extreme disagreement we do so not just from our usual mindless interruptive habits. We interrupt ferociously and fast. And I think the fire with which we interrupt in extreme disagreement signals something fundamental at work.

I think it is the assumption of *core difference* between us. I think it is the lived assumption that the extreme disagreement between us is not just a difference of view; it is a difference of *identity*. It is a difference in the kind of person we are, in our very humanity.

It is an assumption of difference so profound that to approach it with even a tentative question mark is to risk becoming some other identity, someone else, someone inferior to ourselves. To think afresh about an issue by listening with interest to an extreme opposing view feels, therefore, like risking personal annihilation. This assumption of 'core difference' is nothing less than the fear of ceasing to be.

The assumption of 'core difference' seems to be a composite of these subsets:

Who I am is what I believe
I am entirely right and you are entirely wrong
My rightness is proven by my values
My values are superior to yours
Who I am, my deep identity, is set immutably in my superior values
If I become interested in your view, I will have to adopt your values, and so I will stop being me; I will be an inferior person

Polarization emerges as an entrenched living of those assumptions of 'core difference'. It is the state of believing that the view of an issue cannot itself be analysed or objectively considered because to do that is to threaten who we *are*.

I think the cycle may look like this: we hold a passionate view on an issue, a passion that comes from values we hold tremblingly dear, values that define our core. We, therefore, become *afraid* to hear the other person's thoughts because to consider them would be, we feel, to betray our deepest selves. So we make sure that no idea can develop in either of us that does not fit our certainty of who we are and who they are. We stop them. We interrupt.

In the grip of polarization we then are sure that the only thing that can bring about understanding is for the other person to change their view completely. We know they won't. So we give up. We hide. We don't go near those flaming topics with them. We know that conversation aimed at understanding is an utter waste of time. And dangerous to our identity.

This assumption of 'core difference' that both causes and comes from interruption turns us into idiots, wild, unable to create the conditions for new thinking between us because we are not interested *at all* in where the other will go in their thinking. We do not care.

And so it goes.

Wherever we find polarization, we find interruption.

But what I think we have to learn indelibly is that in reality there is no 'core difference' of identity between us. Difference, yes. But 'core difference', as in one of us is more human than the other? I doubt it. There is no difference of being that makes the other person entirely wrong, that makes differing views between us a moral (and mortal) danger to us and to our beloved institutions of respect and equality and dignity. There is no true difference so extreme it should be contraband in our dearest relationships and communities and their place in our hearts.

How do I know? Because I have seen the conviction of 'core difference' dissolve when people are in even a partial thinking environment. And a truth does not dissolve just because humans who hold that truth suddenly treat each other in a new way. Truth is impervious to behaviour. And, as I will illustrate in a moment, I have seen the so-called truth of 'core difference' vanish when people change even one behaviour: they stop interrupting.

I think we have to discard this pull to see the other as different to their core. And we have to recognize the interplay between interruption and this pull. They fortify each other venomously.

Fortification, in fact, is the point. And we need to become literate in the most venal forms of fortification of core identity difference. In particular, we all need to read and absorb the analysis of Michael Hogg, professor and chair of social psychology at Claremont Graduate University (see *Scientific American*, September 2019, pp. 79–81). He shows that a state of 'self-uncertainty social identity' is fodder for the internet 'information nodes' like Twitter and Facebook. These 'I-do-belong-here' platforms keep participants feeding on the amplified disinformation that everyone inside the group is better than everyone outside it, and that only inside are we safe. This repetitive, stupefying experience is its own kind of interruption of independent thinking, if not a killer of it.

So, naivety? You decide. I think we have to face it. Interruption is a killer. It is a killer of connection, of thought, of self. It is a killer of understanding, of esteem, of respect, of accuracy, of imagination.

When we see that, really see it, we stop interrupting. We hold on to the fact that nothing can threaten our identity unless we allow it to. We look around. We gradually become more interested in discovering what the other person cares about and wants and really thinks than we are in walking as sentinels to our *selves*.

When we do, we may begin to think together about our extreme disagreement. We start by listening to understand, not to convince. That can be enough. We start to learn. We begin to see that we were wrong about them. Not wholly. But sufficiently. And they were wrong about us.

We *see*.

Where can this lead?

From this dissolving of the assumption of 'core difference' we can, if we want to, deftly move 'extreme disagreement' into 'creative difference of view' where new ideas can spring up between us that we absolutely could not have conceived before. Our dialogue becomes a true re-thinking, a creation of something that was impossible for either of us inside our terror of losing ourselves.

Soon we agree that our differences can lead us out of conformity and derivation. We remember that humanity's best constructs have come from the transcendent power of thinking together *within* our disagreements, even our extreme ones, not in spite of them.

Bill Godwin, American scientist and philosopher, sees something additional at the heart of polarized entrenchment:

A typical reaction in America today on meeting or reading the writings of someone with a different political or cultural view is to dismiss them at least as ignorant or uninformed or misinformed, if not outright evil. But if one thinks about it, the all-too-common statement, 'I can't see why anyone would be so [dumb, ignorant, misinformed, etc.] as to believe that' is really in fact a statement about our own ignorance. Clearly they do believe what they believe, and they believe it for reasons which seem perfectly sound to them, and if we can't see why they believe what they believe then clearly that reflects some profound ignorance on our own part.

One can react to this basically in three different ways. One can dismiss them and their views out of hand. That is the most comfortable reaction and what most people seem to do, but it just leaves us bound in our own ignorance, perhaps feeling falsely virtuous from our supposedly 'superior' understanding of the world.

One can argue with them, but that just pits our own cultural and life experiences, assumptions and biases against theirs; and since each of us is arguing from within our own different cognitive and emotional framework, arguments seldom change anyone's mind or accomplish anything useful. Still, many people seem to love the emotional high and virtuous feeling that arguments give them.

Or one can freely admit one's ignorance and explore with them respectfully and with an open mind just why they believe what they believe. It is important to do this from a serious commitment on our own part of wanting to learn and understand the other's views, rather than as just an exercise in gathering ammunition for our next assault on them.

One needs to begin with the assumption (obviously true if one thinks about it) that they may well be right and it is we who are wrong because of our own ignorance or assumption or biases or cultural and life experiences. It's amazing what one can learn about other people's lives, other people's experiences, other people's assumptions and biases, and other people's cultures with this approach. And it is amazing how often that new understanding will modify one's own views.

We all probably need to read that once a week.

I do see progress.

I admit that embracing the promise of no interruption in a setting of extreme disagreement is a challenge. But it is worth the skill, the commitment, the discipline. Most of all the discipline, because if generative attention is anything, it is the reiterative decision to stay disciplined. Discipline produces freedom, nearly always. And this act of attention does exactly that. It restores respect where derision had moved in and begun to rot the premises. It liberates.

Could something so simple, so elegant, so perfectly ours, accomplish a big thing like outwitting polarization? Such a big, anciently elusive, incorrigible thing? Could human attention so catalytic it changes cells, this focus of insatiable wondering, of hunger fully to understand, expose the ruse of deep difference, dry up its tubers and let us think again?

Yes. I think so.

We *can* create a thinking environment even in the dwellings of extreme disagreement. We can, quite simply and profoundly, promise not to interrupt. We can honour the three ingredients of that promise: to start giving attention, to stay interested in where the person will go next and to 'share the stage' equally.

We want to do it.

We can do it.

And, blissfully, this promise is up to the job.

And I am confident that supple security in our own identity grounded in the recognition that 'core difference' does not exist, added to our promise not to interrupt, will over time effect the changes all of us want. We will generate ideas we have not thought of yet. And nimbly.

I am confident because I have watched the promise work when the threads of respect frayed. I have seen reconnection repair and regenerate relationship. Most impressively, I have seen fresh thought flow where rage before had ravaged reason.

And this change can happen anywhere.

At work, for example, people navigate this interruptive road to polarization most days. Nick, one of my clients, despaired about this and then solved it:

'My office is full of bright, energetic "millennials". I am "Gen X". Translate those annoying labels to mean that ageism reigns. It almost certainly always has. But now because of these identity "tags", we can see the ageist culture wars for what they are. Translate that to mean that polarization sits tight in our office.

'Last week I asked Ruth, the head of marketing, to stop texting her colleagues about issues and go talk to them instead. She hated that. She argued that it would take more time. She could not see what benefit it could possibly achieve.

'I said it matters that people be in each other's presence, look into each other's eyes, read each other's shifts of feeling and mood during the conversation and really listen to each other, not just react.

'She sighed. She shut up. She said she would do it next time.

'Later, I saw her get up from her desk and walk across the room to her colleague's desk. But she walked in that "for god's sake" way.

'"She just doesn't get it," I thought. "Millennials are different. They have these human-connection bypasses." I figured she had a similar summing-up of me: "Gen X equals tech-impaired." I am completely right. You are completely wrong. Who I *am* is at stake here. I am not budging.'

Nick sighed. He was quiet a long time. Then he looked up. 'I just realized,' he said, 'that in every encounter I have had with Ruth we have interrupted each other. And the conversations inevitably ground into dominance and compliance. In the end, because of the power differential, I had "won". But I had lost, too. The battles still raged.'

Nick then decided to change one thing. He would use his power next time to require the promise of no interruption between them: for attention from and for each other, for at least some interest in where the other would go next with his thoughts and for approximately equal turns between them to think and speak. And he would say that the point of the conversation was not to convince each other, but to understand each other on the issue. He would start with a turn each to say what mattered to them about the issue. Then they would each say what they really thought on the issue itself. They would not interrupt. No matter what.

It worked. Nick said that the biggest change was immediate: there was less fear in the room. The promise of no interruption does exactly that: it defuses the fear. In its place, gradually, is safety. And from safety grows better thinking and clearer conveying of thought and feeling. And from that grows understanding, and from that the threat of polarization shrinks.

It was not a miracle, and it took some months for this promise of no interruption (with its three ingredients) to edge towards the centre of their office culture, but gradually it happened.

★

And in gatherings?

I have seen similar depolarizing in groups on political issues. (Each time I work with people with polarized political views, I think we should reverse the 1970s maxim to read: *The political is personal*.)

As I write this, I am sitting in a world whose political polarization is so livid, it seems a phenomenon unique in human history. But it is not. Polarization has always stalked us. You need be only a casual reader of history to know that. But perhaps because there are more ways these days to broadcast with violence the extreme disagreements between us, because a single thought can go viral to millions of people in a second, we are battered more steadily by our awareness of it, and so we feel sicker longer and for more days of the week. But political polarization is far from new. And functionally it is no different from the polarization in Nick's office. Its resolution is the same as well.

I saw this inspiringly and in an unlikely place. Once a month five couples from Burleson, Texas, gather to create a thinking environment. They talk and think together about things that matter to them. They promise not to interrupt: they give attention; they stay interested in where the person speaking will go with their thoughts; they 'share the stage' with equal turns.

They do this in pairs and in rounds and in discussion. Two hours later they leave more deeply connected to their spouse and to each other.

They have been doing this every month for twenty-five years. I was their original teacher and occasional facilitator over the years. (They affectionately call it 'Nancy's Gang', a label I failed to combat.) I grew more and more moved by what they achieved, and by just the fact that they kept meeting. I am impressed if a group lasts twenty-five minutes, never mind twenty-five years.

So for this twenty-fifth anniversary celebration, they again invited me to facilitate. And I decided to take a chance. I asked them to do a brave thing: to talk about something apparently terrifyingly taboo among them. In their monthly meetings for more than two years there had been a 'great undiscussable roaming creature' in the room: the country's leader.

For twenty-three of those twenty-five years of meeting, this group had been able to talk about anything. Anything. That is one thing they cherished about the group. But then this person announced his candidacy and instantly became the first thing the group could not talk about.

Two whole years had gone by. Still no mention of the prominence of this topic. In that time a few of the pro-him people told me they were sure exactly who the anti-him people were in the group, and what they thought, and that there was no point in discussing their views given that the anti-him people were 100 per cent wrong. The anti-him people told me the converse. Both were sure they knew all they needed to know about the others' views, and that conversation was pointless and, probably, dangerous. A few said they were furious. A few said they were frightened.

But they agreed to open it up with me and to trust the promise of no interruption even with this incandescent topic.

We gathered. We confirmed the promise of no interruption with its three ingredients, and the intention to embody all ten components of a thinking environment, if possible.

We started with the usual opening round. Opening rounds create psychological safety because everyone remembers that they matter equally and because the experience is appreciative and full of ease. This time the question focused on what the group meant to them twenty-five years on.

Then we did a round on this question:

On the subject of this leader, what matters most to you?

Everyone had three minutes to think and speak. I was pretty sure that round would be important. But it was transformatively so.

In fact, I was about to set up the next round when one of the anti-him people spoke. 'I think,' she said gently, 'we need to pause and acknowledge what has just happened here. We are palpably different than we were thirty minutes ago. I seem just like everyone else, even though I know that on this subject I am not like many of you. I feel connected to everyone at some level of shared being, a level that matters more than the differences. I am not scared any more. And yet my political views have not changed. It is as if each of us has let the other in. Something has happened. I am not sure what it is. But even if this is all we did here, it would have been worth the whole day.'

Everyone – everyone – nodded.

We started the next round. The question was:

On the subject of this leader, what more do you think, or feel, or want to say?

Each person had five minutes.

There was fervour this time; people's emotional connection to their views was deeply personal. And at a few points I sensed they were holding on for dear life to the promise not to interrupt. In those moments the promise seemed to be the only thing between them and disintegration of the person's turn and the whole group's integrity. For me these moments are reassuring, not alarming. The promise is rugged and soon reinstates the ingredients of attention and interest.

And because the promise in that way holds back the touchpaper of adrenaline and cortisol, the grounding of serotonin and oxytocin gradually increase, and those near-death moments subside. The speaker keeps thinking, and the others start again to understand, and even to learn.

From there people can risk factoring in to their view a few bits of the other's view, knowing somewhere without words that their own identity is safe and sometimes even that their own identity can branch out a bit, consider this or that additional perspective, develop a new does-this-fit nuance. The fear of losing who we are at our core no longer calls the shots. Our freed minds do.

That is what happened. All of that. Some of it they spoke about later. Some they could not find words for but said they could feel. Visibly and movingly, the censoring was over. There was no longer staked terrain. Only open ground.

*

I also have seen polarization dissolve in learning groups. It is not easy for people in groups, having painstakingly developed safety, then to call forth the delicate, unsaid things among them. But by confirming the promise of no interruption and by establishing a robust thinking environment, facing and then defacing polarization is possible. It can happen if everyone speaks in turn, or with a demonstration between two people in dialogue.

On the topic of abortion, for example, two people in dialogue moved from distrust and fear to understanding and respect, in twenty-four minutes. That was certainly not a certainty going in because the pro-life person was a man; the pro-choice person, a woman. And the woman had said that 'Men should not be part of the abortion debate. End of.'

Each had three minutes to speak. We had taken ten minutes at the start to review the agreements and the promise, and then for each to say in a three-minute turn what the topic meant to them.

The dialogue question did the rest:

On the subject of abortion, what do you think, or feel, or want to say?

The remarkable thing was not just that after three turns each the level of tension dropped and the connection between them restored noticeably, or even that they occasionally laughed, and never shouted. What was amazing was what one of them said about it at the end: 'I started this wary, even distrustful. But now, although she has not changed her view, I feel close to her.' The other said she felt a similar change.

Sometimes new thought, not just new understanding, emerges from a depolarizing dialogue like this. Again, with a group observing, two people had a dialogue, this time about climate change. One described herself as a 'climate warrior'. The other as 'questioning the whole thing'. They addressed the same questions with the same agreements and time frames.

About halfway through the thirty-six minutes, they agreed not to nod so much, noting that when we nod almost all of the time, we seem to rush each other, and rushing makes us tense and slows down our thinking. So they stopped nodding and let their calm faces and eyes communicate respect and interest. Suddenly one of them was quiet for a few seconds while the other continued to listen. Out of the quiet the person said, 'I think I do understand something here.' She articulated the other's point and then moved it further where neither of them had been before.

There was not complete agreement between them. But there was some. They smiled as it ended. They now understood each other for the first time. That had just never happened before. It had been challenging. But second by second it had borne emotional fruit, increments of ease, allowing the content of their thinking to progress and improve.

They had demonstrated that in the end humans want to be understood more than we want to win. The earth between them now was tilled.

27. Just Like You

I've been thinking about all of this. About what happens when the promise not to interrupt depolarizes people because it dissolves the delusion of 'core difference'. I am thinking that it may be the embrace of this paradox:

I am not like you. I am just like you.

It is a salient and discomfiting truth – for our work, for our dear relationships, for our schools and our religions and, certainly, as we have seen, our politics.

I am not like you. I am just like you.

How can both be true at once? They just can. They just are. Life is like that: maddeningly and mercifully paradoxical. In fact, nested inside this paradox is another one: *we are the same, but difference is all there is.* We are different inside our sameness. The strong and deadly pull, though, is to think we see difference in our *humanity* when all we are seeing is difference in our *experience.* When we give in to this societal pull to dehumanize, we pull away from each other, judging, condemning, ostracizing. This we can stop.

'I tried it,' said one of my colleagues. 'I caught myself looking at a stranger the other day. She was "a mess". Everything she wore was thrown on. Fat blocked her view of the floor. Her arm was a lawn of tattoos. She chewed gum and popped it. She spoke loudly into her phone about the jerk at work. And she said, "me and her did it". I disdained all of that. I was raised to.'

I thought to myself that no one actually told her to, of course. But our deepest learning is never uttered. We infer it from eyebrows and speed of head-turning.

'But this time,' she continued, 'I remembered: *I am not like you; I am just like you.*

'And honestly,' she said, 'it seemed as if my entire unconscious childhood just stood up and left the building. Epiphany-like, it opened my inner eyes. I could see her. *Her*. Not my idea of her. I began to wonder in a kind of excited way what she cared about and what she hoped for and why she was right here at this moment and where she was going. I wondered about *her*.

'I started to imagine how we are just alike. Things matter to us both very much, even if they are not the same things. We both are afraid of things, maybe even of the same things, like betrayal and prejudice (including our own). Maybe we both like to sing. Or write. Or smell a gardenia. And for sure we both want to love. I began to like her. Who I was was no longer defined by distancing from who I thought she was. And if she were to speak to me about something, I would now want to understand her, on any subject.

'That was nice,' she said, 'but it was also alarming. It mattered, and I wanted to race right out and look afresh at everyone in my life and in my past whose way of being was so different from mine it petrified me. I wanted to find out what they thought about things and really begin to understand them.'

We talked for a long time about that. We agreed about the intelligent power in that paradox:

I am not like you. I am just like you.

This resolvable contradiction, when internalized, allows us to nurture our own identities and simultaneously enter the identity of someone else by letting go of identity altogether. As we have seen, it is in the nature of paradox to produce another one. Our brains love them.

28. Giving It Up

How then can we start? What comes first to move into a state of 'creative difference' where fresh and nourishing thinking, and even change, can happen? How can we prevent these identity-infused disconnections from each other?

Immediately, as we have seen, *we* can stop interrupting. That act alone can prevent disconnection and then polarization from setting in, and it can diffuse it if it gets going.

Additionally, though, I would go much further. I would propose that we step back and think afresh about identity itself.

I propose we look soberly beneath these human constructs of identity and see that there is nothing there, that it is all made up. Our identities are our creations. They are our *inventions*, not our nature. They are the socialized product of our experience and learning, of serendipity and coincidence, even of oppression itself.

In that way as humans we *construct* the idea of identity. Then we slip into it. Then we bond with it. Then we sharpen the difference between our identity and others'. Then we reason that both identities cannot be right, and so the different person or view has to be wrong, and, therefore, that view is a threat to us. So we turn the 'other' identity, the 'non-us' identity, into the enemy of our very being. And we cannot think independently together for a second.

I think we need a way out of this.

I think we need to see that we are only wondrous humans there under all identities, longing to think outside them, all the way to something good for *everyone*. We are in there, waiting to think for ourselves – together. Not perfectly, but well enough to keep going. Well enough gradually to devise together an even better path ahead. Well enough to allow us to align. We do not even have to agree. If we can align, our differences, free of identity, will enrich us.

And I would go even further. I would ask whether in seeing the self-constructed nature of our identities, we could consider giving them up altogether. Could we strip away the 'I am' and replace it with 'I believe' or 'I do' or 'I care about' or 'I want' or 'I hope for'?

Instead of describing ourselves in nouns or adjectives – 'I am a liberal', 'I am a conservative' – we would use verbs to say what we mean: 'I want a smaller pay gap between the top and the bottom' or 'I want small government'.

I just wonder what might happen if in that way we actually brooked no identities at all except 'human being'. How would we then respond to difference?

A thinking environment is by its very nature a respite from identity, from its imposition on our seeing of the 'other' and of the world. We are invited to think *as* ourselves so that we can think *for* ourselves.

But who are ourselves? Who are we really? Are we only the history and present experience of prejudice? Conversely, are we only the historical and present achievements of people who are roughly our skin colour or sex or nationality? Is that who we *are*?

We are whatever genetically generated designs compel us in one direction or another. But are we accurately the easy-to-label history of our current or ancient oppression? We inhabit a world of prejudice, and we fight with all our intelligent might to change its structures and attitudes. But is that who we are? Is that our identity? Are we the labels? Or are we human beings who value, who experience certain things?

So I wonder. What might happen if we were to consider no longer labelling ourselves or each other? What might change if we thought and spoke in the actual rather than the abstract?

And without easy-to-label identity and without the threat of identity death, what might happen to interruption? And then to our thinking? And then to polarization?

Because our identities spring from our lived life, we are in charge of them. We do not have to hold on to them for dear life. We can choose to let them wander around in someone else's identity for a few minutes, inspecting its joins and its aspect, and then go home if we want.

Or we can stay for supper. If we stay, we can sometimes go home later with a greater knowledge of our own joins.

And sometimes with windows in new places.

29. Expanding Intelligence

I find when human nature and its society seem too vast to grasp, I need to stumble upon comets of profound insight. That happened for me recently in the thinking of Humberto Maturana. He is a Chilean biologist and philosopher. He said this:

> Love, allowing the other to be a legitimate other, is the only emotion that expands intelligence.

You can imagine my excitement when a colleague sent me that quotation. Frankly, I think it is so beautiful, so kaleidoscopically resettling, so deftly catapulting of us into a fresh understanding of our whole species that I still hardly know what to do with myself when I read it. I wrote an essay on it. That helped for a few months. But now I am back to wondering how else to shout it from all the rooftops in the world.

So to stay within the purview of this book, I will say just this: maybe polarization is exactly that – the delegitimizing of the 'other' and the consequent reducing of intelligence.

It makes sense. People chewed up by polarization do look stupid. They do look and behave as if their intelligence is not all it used to be. They have, as we have seen, probably assumed their core identity is in danger and have squeezed it to their chests so fiercely it gasps. And their brains, bleeding oxygen, assume there is a core difference between them and the person with the 'absolutely completely wrong' view. They simply cannot listen to them for fear of the death of their entire self. Of course they seem stupid.

Conversely, I love the idea that to allow the 'other' to be a legitimate other is to grow smarter. And if we can grow smarter, we have a better chance of creating new ways forward, *together*. If we can do that, we can all eventually have good lives. *All* of us.

But again that state of a-good-life-for-us-all is going to take new thinking. New thinking takes intelligence. Intelligence takes legitimizing the other. Legitimizing the other takes the mutual experience of respect. Respect takes the promise of no interruption.

I cherish the conclusion this produces: the promise not to interrupt legitimizes the other, makes us smarter and is an act of love.

Love, allowing the other to be a legitimate other, is the only emotion that expands intelligence.

Thank you, Maturana.
And the system of polarization?
One day, I predict, nowhere to be found.

30. Centaur

All four systems of interruption reinforce each other. The systems of digistraction and polarization, however, also *seed* each other in ways we need to understand.

Again, our digital platforms purport to connect us. But at any significant level they mostly separate us. Posts particularly. Posts are not real connections. They are airings. They can be delightful, and they keep each other in mind; but they do not allow us truly to be present. And so they do not allow us to think with each other.

By design they disallow 'readings' of faces, of tones, of posture, of pace, of pause. Those 'readings', when we are in person or even through FaceTime or Zoom and its cousins, even on the phone, force us at least to face the real-time effects of what we are saying, and require us to take responsibility for what we say next. And so it is entirely predictable that on digital-posting platforms, including the single-dimension email platform, people say things they just would not say if they had to witness or hear the effects on the recipient of their words as they deliver them.

Of course, we say horrible things to each other in person. But there is an instant feedback loop that tells us to stop. If we defy it, we witness the painful result instantly. We know we are doing damage. And that picture of pain usually pulls us back, and eventually stops us. We see the human being we are assaulting. We see the blood we are spilling. And that does something to us.

The disembodied nature of posts, however, wherever they are, disconnects us from the other's pain. And as we all know from the research and from experience, the apps that have 'likes' *make* us, again by design, particularly pathetic prey. Because self-esteem can begin to depend on how many 'likes' we have, we become ravenous for that artificial, ephemeral approval. The 'virality' design of platform life also compounds the pain. The more people see our stuff, the more we care what they think. There is nothing real about 'likes'. It is not meaningful respect or admiration, nor is the absence of 'likes' meaningful disrespect or exclusion. It is platform numbness caused by platform non-connection. And yet we live it as real. And we defend it.

Crucial in all of this is that it is not just the posts and pictures that go viral. It is, long term more devastatingly, the interruption of our independent thinking that goes viral. Interruption online is becoming the lived culture. It is so lived, in fact, that not only is it unquestioned, it is unseen.

Enter polarization. Polarization is the perfect plaything of the posting platform. They were made (somewhere not in heaven) for each other. They are really two beasts in one. The posts can proliferate polarization. And it is not just that posts have the go-viral capacity. It is subtler than that.

As we have seen, polarization deepens with *disconnection*. So posts, exactly because they disconnect us from each other, can turn disagreement into disconnection.

Soon, because of this disconnection, we begin to feel the imagined threat to our very identity, fuelling fear of our core's disappearing, and then rage at the 'disappearer'. The rage disconnects us further, producing out-of-control sending/receiving/reacting/sending/reacting/sending non-thinking, non-thoughtful, non-really-us disconnection into the non-world of self-perpetuating interruption.

We could instead warn each other of these interlocking forms of disappearance, as we warn each other of other platform perils. It is good, for example, that we alert each other to the porn, paedophilia and general 'stranger danger' traps lurking on various platform posts. But perhaps we should be warning each other about the platforms themselves.

We could help each other to understand first that the platform's design *disconnects* us from meaningful interaction with each other, and then, because the platform is *designed* to keep us on it for as long as possible and to return as soon as possible, we spend more and more of our days disconnected, from the people on the platform and from the people we are not being with in person because we spend so much time on the platform.

For me the huge question, one that in my view is as pressing as any, including climate change, is this pervasive and ignorantly accepted trio of interruption, digistraction and polarization, that strips the self off its bones and tears us away from each other.

We have created with our fine minds the very means to destroy their fineness. And I wonder where this will go.

Clearly then, interruption is more than stopping someone from continuing to talk. It is more than destroying a person's silence. It is more than slipping our clever remark into the middle of someone's sentence or, worse, finishing their sentence for them. It is also the very construct of commerce, of communication, of convincing and of contention that are the norms directing lives.

We purchase everything as a pawn inside this entity-owned, conglomerate, no-choice, conformonomics, 'nothing' system of doing business.

We pick up our phone before we open our eyes and kneel all day at its digistraction feet of platform pings and banners and 'likes'.

We attach ourselves passionately to ideas and people because we do not see the kill shots and repetition, unpredictability, cognitive dissonance and reassignation of trust for the persuasion ruse they are.

And we weaken into the easy but wholly wrong assumption that if we listen to certain views, we lose who we are; and so we lose sight of each other, and then we inflame dialogue, polarized more with every post.

All of this is interruption. Because all of it interrupts us as thinkers.

I can imagine something different. I can imagine us someday listening to each other worldwide, family-wide, friend-wide, work-wide. I can. I have seen dependable glimpses of this. They thrill me every time.

This is a simple, complex, consequential change. And we can make it.

31. Emergency: When Interruption is Good

Long before this page you have surely been protesting that there *are* times when interruption is okay. Even necessary. And I agree. Fully. We certainly don't want a society of on-and-on-and-ons until we keel over and give up listening altogether. And we don't want to allow abuse to continue for any reason, at any age, at any time, neither from parents nor presidents. And we don't want to let babies cry themselves to sleep alone, turning them into need junkies as adults because they internalized that their needs cannot be met. And we don't want lies to embed. Under those and similar circumstances, we have to interrupt.

But that's about it. Otherwise, we can let the person finish at least their sentence, at best their thought. Even if their information is wrong, or they are plotting something illegal or unethical, or they are saying something that may be perpetuating prejudice, or they are betraying their agreement to be proportional in their turn, or as the listener our body is growing uncomfortable, we can listen to the end of their sentence (assuming their favourite orator is not Joyce). No one is going to die. And we will be better informed at the end of it.

But, most importantly, they will be able to *think* about our 'correction' or even our decision to withdraw from the dialogue if we need to, or our warning that we will have to report their nefarious plans to the authorities if they continue, if we do not assault them by interrupting. And in those moments you definitely do want them to be able to think well as you speak. The guideline for me in whether to interrupt or not is whether the interruption will gain more for clear, independent thinking than will the intact dignity of the person after they have completed their thought.

So 'emergency' is probably a good gauge.

And actually, I would argue that interruption itself is the biggest emergency of all. Interruption is the thing we *must* interrupt. It is our society at war with itself. It is the invader of independent thinking.

We *can* interrupt interruption. At any moment we can stop people when they stop us. We can also make the promise of no interruption the agreed culture of our relationships and our organizations.

Nothing could be simpler in the world.

PART THREE

Understanding the Promise

32. From Birth to Death

'What is your vision?'

Sometimes people ask me that. Then they ask me what my strategy is, then my plan, then my next steps, then my accountability structure, then my performance indicators. Really? I don't think they have heard that micro-planning is out. 'Out' happens to things that actually don't work. And telling the future exactly what to do is hopeless.

Don't get me wrong, I'm a planner. I love to make lists and mind-mappy things with the main focus in the middle and subsets floating around it inside little clouds. And I like to make 'do next' lists (I even have a 'next next' list). I feel good after I have made those.

But I no longer kid myself. Not all that much turns out exactly the way I planned. My plans guide, and that's good; but they don't guarantee. And that's fine.

Visions are different, though. To accomplish anything amounting to a dream, we need a vision, and we need a supple strategy to get us there over time. So I have a vision, and the simplest ever strategy. But no detailed plan, no time-lined steps, no agreements with people to call me once a week to be sure I am on target. And I certainly never put numbers to my performance. Contrary to the current worship of numbers to size up what matters, I think the most significant things humans long for and experience probably cannot be measured. A vision needs way more room than that.

My vision is that one day people will live in a thinking environment from birth to death. My strategy is to notice what helps people to think for themselves, and to share that. (That is a single strategy because noticing and sharing entirely depend on each other.)

I focus on this here because that vision is the natural fulfilment of the promise not to interrupt. And the strategy seems to be working. Slowly. Imperfectly. Which is perfect.

By a 'thinking environment from birth to death' I mean that a person would be 'baptized' at birth with the promise from their entire society not to interrupt them or their thinking (except in said emergencies). That would, of course, mean that from the very first minute of life they would experience generative attention from their mother, and from every adult who held them or played with them or cared for them in any way. As they got older, a frequently asked question in their life would be, 'What do you think?' Not instead of warranted, wise authority and informed guidance and the richness of reasonable cultural constructs, of course, but in addition to them.

It would mean that they would be experiencing this kind of attention and equality everywhere: in the cradle, at child care, in primary school and secondary school and university and graduate school, among friends and with first and second and forever lovers, at worship, in therapy, in coaching, and in every minute of work including meetings and presentations, and on the new non-interruptive, deeply connected non-platform-platforms, and at the new creativity-rich and skin-in-the-game market places, and back at home each night, and on holiday and in retirement and whenever ill, and when dying.

Right up to the end they would have lived in a world in which interruption was so rare it was weird, in which every human mind was valued, where formerly intractable societal problems were gradually reversed because brand-new ideas had been able to bud and ripen, and tyrannies of every sort were easy to subdue because people were not.

That is my vision.

And the disarmingly simple strategy 'to notice and share' is to stay alert to what is happening when people seem to be thinking well for themselves, and then to share that. To keep noticing, even (especially) when it entails throwing out what we observed before because a new 'noticing' has made the other one obsolete, even wrong. And to keep sharing. And noticing.

That's it. Vision and strategy. It's a description, not a prescription. But asking yourself boldly what you most want and thinking for yourself about how in broad terms to make it unfold seems to be a good thing. Most people don't realize their dreams because there are no hard questions in the vision, and nothing sufficiently generative in the strategy.

And there is way too much planning. For one thing, too much controlled planning makes it impossible for 'that's funny' to happen in our lives. 'That's funny' is the saviour of right and the wrecker of wrong. I love the 'that's funny' moments in history. It is that famous Asimov moment when, after decades, having tidied up your theory and gotten it into the world, having been recognized as the genius you are, having published and lectured all over the world, you notice something.

'That's funny,' you think.

At first you shrug. Then you look away. Then with one eye you look back. It is still there. It doesn't disappear even when you tilt things and roll them around.

By dawn the theory collapses. Seeing has started. Something new, and sometimes glorious, is about to emerge.

Our world, I would argue, has far too few 'that's funny' moments. We interrupt too much. We interrupt each other's thinking with dogma, unexamined convention and the ever-revered 'latest thinking'. 'That's funny' doesn't have a chance.

We need 'that's funny' in abundance. The inconsistencies between theory and practice are out there, all set to produce those moments. We've already seen masses of inconsistencies highlighted in Part Two of this book. Every system of interruption reeks of them. Economics is supposed to liberate, but it subjugates. Digital life is supposed to focus, but it distracts. Persuasion is supposed to lead, but it inveigles. Identity is supposed to recognize, but it polarizes. That's funny.

So when we make this promise not to interrupt each other or ourselves, we cannot plan where it will take us. We have to be okay with that. We have to hold on to the vision of human independent thinking and let go of knowing what's coming. We cannot plan our way to new ideas. Our minds won't allow it. They are looking too hard for 'that's funny'. *We* need to be, too.

To do that, we need rigorously to *understand* the promise of no interruption. To do that we must take a look at the things it changes.

There are hundreds. I have chosen five. They pervade our world, and they are proving robust. I am following them with interest.

See what you think.

33. When It Matters Most

When I was twenty-six, the doctors said I would be dead in six weeks. They had found ovarian cancer metastasized throughout my abdomen. They removed what they could. The rest would kill me.

They offered me a 'special' place on a chemotherapy trial at the National Institutes of Health in Washington. They said that would give me a 20 per cent chance of living five years.

While I was in hospital, Peter, my husband of only four months, began to research my options. There was no internet. There was no Google. There was the Library of Congress; there were encyclopaedias; there were journals; there were experts; there were survivors and there was the telephone. He used them all.

As he learned things, he shared them with me.

Other things happened, too, that I now see as pieces of a whole, but then just experienced and contemplated casually.

Probably most important was that he met with every member of my family and told them I would have a chance of living if they would believe I could, and if they would be only positive around me, supporting whatever approach I took for healing. They promised. I do not know what fears or doubts that promise had to subdue, but to this day I cannot remember a flicker of doubt in a single eye.

And that was only the beginning. Each morning, for example, Peter came to my room with a suitcase of fresh food he had prepared for me, eating the hospital's fare himself before the nurse came back. What I did not know was that he had instructed my sister and her husband to buy these healthful foods and get them ready for him to bring to me.

Early on my twin came to visit me, summoned from his action in Vietnam. I was still in a drugged haze, but we had a sweet conversation. He stayed a long time. I dozed. When I woke, he was standing next to my bed, his hands above my abdomen, his eyes closed. Suddenly in a jolt he fell back into the chair by the bed. I did not understand that. But I was profoundly comforted by his presence.

A few days later Peter invited Dr William F. C. Chao, a Taiwanese ovarian oncologist who was lecturing in the States, to visit me on my surgeon's day off. Dr Chao examined me. Then he said, 'I can heal you with my herbs. But if you decide against that, be sure to do this: be happy, happy, happy.'

The next day, in the late evening, I woke in the semi-dark to a gentle whisper. 'Nancy, this is your uncle Henry Bennet. I am a gynaecological, oncological surgeon. Your slides are bad. But I have seen other women with cancer this severe, and as many lived who just went home as who did chemotherapy.' He kissed my forehead. And left.

About a week into my stay, my father, who had come with my mother from New Mexico, asked me to take a walk with him down the hall. I have told that story in *Time To Think* and in a Lloyd Wigglesworth vimeo, so I will not retell it here. But I will say that during the near purity with which my father on that walk listened to me, mostly to my silence, without a breath of interruption, I knew that I would live.

Anticipating my return home in a few days, Peter called all of our friends. We had twenty-seven. He told them about the cancer and the prognosis. And he asked them if they could have faith that I would live. He said that if they said no, we would ask that they not visit me. Eight said yes.

The day before I left the hospital Peter and I began to share our thinking. We were going to have to tell the surgeon and his team the next day whether we would accept their invitation to join the NIH trials.

Slowly, I had come to a personal view of cancer. From the little I knew about it, I reasoned that it had not 'flown' into my body from the outside, like a germ or a bacterium. So I thought my body had probably made the cancer from the inside. If so, it could unmake it from the inside. In fact, I thought it would have unmade it when the cancer cells first developed, if its natural cells for healing had not been disabled, if the environment that nurtures them had been operating properly.

I also figured that the cells that comprise the body's healing environment, as with all its other functions, must be affected by what *we* do to the body. And there seemed to me logically to be six main categories of things we do that probably affect the body on a regular basis: we eat and drink; we think; we feel; we exercise; we have conviction; we love.

I did not at the time understand technically how those things could affect the cells of the body, but it seemed reasonable that they would, because each of them generated a physiological response in my body that I could detect. And they did so in the bodies of everyone else I knew, too.

Therefore, if those categories of things were having an ongoing impact on my body's cells that were responsible for nipping any cancer that popped up, I thought I would need to identify what I was doing habitually in each of those categories and start doing something different. I would need to start doing something more likely to help that system in some way. I would need to do all of them because, I was sure, nothing operates in isolation; everything affects everything else.

So my system of dying would have to be replaced with a system of living. I understood later that of course this system of living is the human immune system. As a society we know a lot more about that now. Thank goodness.

Anyway, Peter said that he had assembled an array of documents for me to study. 'Whatever you think and whatever you decide, we will do,' he said.

On the last morning the doctors came to my room. They re-issued the invitation for me to join the NIH trial. They said it would be crucial for me to begin within two weeks, given the speed of the remaining cancer growth inside me.

I said, 'Thank you. I appreciate all of that very much. But I am going to decline. I am going to "just go home". I am going to drink carrot juice, cry, jog, live my dreams, believe in my future, be loved and be happy, happy, happy.'

My surgeon smiled. 'If that's what you do, you will be dead in six weeks,' he said.

I went home. I read the books and journals and case studies and personal stories Peter had assembled. I talked with our trusted health and medical advisers. I talked with Peter. And I decided. I would see if my body could restore its own healing system. I changed what I ate, what I did with my life, what I felt, how I exercised, how much conviction I had in my future and who my friends were. I cried and laughed and wrote a book about dance. And I let in love.

Forty-eight years later, reflecting gratefully on these 2,500 weeks of gifted life, I think I understand the source of the clarity of those two weeks of decision: I was not interrupted.

Peter had never interrupted me, neither my talking nor my thinking. He had gathered and shared information. Then he had listened. My father in his different way had done the same. And because that had allowed me to think outside the death prognosis frame, the medical system had not interrupted me either. I had been in a thinking environment from beginning to end.

There is another crucial piece here. The thinking I had to do to make my decision depended on interconnection. It depended on a recognition of the intimate inextricability of all things. It depended on a deep recognition that life is not linear, a recognition that life is a nearly unfathomable complexity of ever-moving interdependent intertwinings of thing and context, of thing and environment.

John Muir, the most famous US conservationist from the nineteenth and twentieth centuries, said it better:

When we try to pick out anything by itself, we find it hitched to everything else in the Universe.

Specifically, when we know we will not be interrupted, when the attention in front of us is driven by a desire to know where we will go next with our thinking, we go organically to interconnection. We leave the thinking silos so beloved by the controlling, moulding, smouldering systems of interruption. And we see new connections.

We ask questions that arise from those connections. Without the promise of no interruption we are too much on alert to the imminent disruption of our thought, and our thought stays safe in its linear trek. We need the promise and the attention to venture off into the tall grass where the missing secrets are.

Life cannot be separated from itself.

'Non-linear' is a beautiful concept. It is, of course, bludgeoned into near oblivion by our systems of interruption that require us desperately not to think afresh outside the systems themselves. But 'non-linear' rises up to greet us the minute we step into the no-interruption promise and its thinking environment.

I think it works like this. We face an issue. We decide to think for ourselves. We secure the promise. We settle in. Suddenly, we can see dimensions of the problem we had not seen. We can see its interlocking components and their logic. We can see the parts moving. We leap from the original context to a different one. We hear their conversations. We see a glint on a missing piece across the field. We see, coming into focus, a new, unexpected and 'just right' path ahead. For me, the most intriguing characteristic of the powerful promise not to interrupt is exactly that it unlocks this interlocking, non-linear perceiving bit of our minds. When we start thinking truly for ourselves, we start thinking non-linearly.

I don't understand right now how it does that. But one day someone will explain it. That happened with the neuroscience of the general experience of the promise (about which more in the next chapter). So I am looking forward to a similarly enlightening explanation of this specific change spawned by the promise of no interruption: non-linear thinking.

I have told this story here not because what I did in the face of a death sentence is what anyone else should do. Nor even because what I did is what saved my life. In fact, I don't even know for sure that I am free of cancer. I actually suspect that we all have cancers growing here and there much of the time, but our immune systems, if nurtured properly, quash them. What I do know is that I am not dead. And whether that is post hoc or propter hoc, I am here.

I tell my story also because I think it is a feature of what a thinking environment from birth to death would produce. And understanding the promise means understanding that it changes even the moments when life is at stake. It changes the way we navigate them and the decisions that come from them, because it allows us to think for ourselves.

I would guess that all of this would be business as usual in a world of no interruption.

34. Thinking Pairs

This promise, as we have seen, can change the very way we live our lives. It can change the way we approach every issue and make every decision. It shows us that everything we decide depends on the quality of the independent thinking we do first, and so it can lead us to set up 'official' thinking times. We want those thinking times because we know they work so astonishingly well.

So in a world in which the promise of no interruption were the culture from birth to death, I suspect everyone would make sure they had these special times for generative attention and focused, independent thinking. They might meet with a 'thinking partner' every day, for example, and progress an issue of their choice so that the rest of their day would go more smoothly and happily and productively, and over time their life would, too. And then they would listen to their thinking partner, who would progress an issue of their choice, too. Both would know that even five minutes each to think for themselves could accomplish all of those amazing things.

They might call those times 'thinking pairs'. I do. And even though our world at the moment is miles away from being a thinking environment from birth to death, many people, after a big heave-ho of habits and an equal amount of undeterrable determination, do now have these thinking pairs every day. In that way the promise of no interruption is changing how we tackle issues in our lives, and how we resurrect joy.

But why would you?

Let me put it this way. How much is a saving of three hours, or thirty days, or two years worth to you? How much is a fresh injection of self-respect, of true connection, of contribution to another's life worth to you? How much is the replacing of anxiety with ease and the lowering of your shoulders worth? How much the enlivening of your relationships? And what about the steady improving of your thinking?

If you thought you could achieve all of that in fifteen minutes a day, would you invest?

What else do you do in a day that takes fifteen minutes? Wait on hold for the next available representative? Check your phones? Look for your keys? Fight with the person you love most in the world? Delete emails? Rehearse the affront you've nursed for seven months? Creep forward in the tailback?

Those don't do a thing for your self-respect, or your deep human connections, or the changing of someone's life as well as your own, or the building of ease and the dropping of the shoulders. And they certainly do not make you a better thinker.

But fifteen minutes a day of a 'thinking pair' will. Guaranteed.

Fifteen minutes every day. Three minutes to say hello and get settled. Five minutes to think. Five minutes to listen. Two minutes to appreciate a quality in each other and say goodbye. Done.

The objective is to think for yourself as far as you possibly can, inside the promise of no interruption, for five whole minutes about a topic or issue of your choice. That may not sound like much time to accomplish all of the glories I mentioned above. But five minutes with this promise is 27.27 times longer than you are likely to get listened to at any other time of your day about anything. And it is just long enough – because there is no interruption to slow down your thinking – to make real progress on something, and to feel like a good, smart and valuable person. Which you are.

The idea is to go as far as you can, for yourself, on the cutting edge of the issue, and along the way to experience the knowledge that you matter profoundly, as only uninterrupted, generative attention can provide. And from that, no matter what insights arise on the topic, no matter what practical outcomes result, ease settles in, and so does greater health and a bit of all-day joy. With that level of return on your investment, it is practically self-mutilation not to do it.

And that's only what happens for you in *your* turn to think. What happens in theirs is just as profound for you. You can tell that you are making a difference to them, that your attention and interest in where they will go next with their thinking, your unverbalized warmth and respect, and your keeping the promise so they are not on guard against your imminent destruction of their next thought are producing valuable thinking and embedding the self-respect and gratitude you experienced with their uninterrupted attention five minutes before.

All of that is why. What could be sweeter?

You can invite a friend, or a colleague, or even a reasonably affable acquaintance to do this with you. Or you could spread the fun and have several different thinking partners.

Whom do you invite? Can it be your spouse or partner? Convenient, I know, but requiring meticulous set-up and boundaries so clean they squeak. It has been done and beautifully. Some couples have a thinking pair first thing, some last thing. And the deepening of the relationship is unmistakable. But the drop-out rate is pretty high. The listener's investment in the outcome of the person's thinking can be all too easily triggered. So, not a bad idea. Just tricky.

Can it be your child? Probably not. The power differential in that relationship is innate, and almost impossible to overcome. And equality is necessary to make a thinking pair work. I know that what we mean by the component of 'equality' is the assumption of equality as *thinkers*, not positional equality. But the parent/child positional power phenomenon is so loaded it warps the requirement for both people to listen to anything the other wants to think about. I do know three mother/daughter thinking pairs that work gorgeously. Both people in the pairs are highly, highly skilled at this; they are both adults; and they don't live together. All of that seems to be crucial.

Can it be your boss? Usually not great. Ditto above. When the practical or emotional investment in the outcome of a thinking pair is potentially high, the chances of its working are potentially low. And with independent thinking you just never know what territory it will wander aimfully into. So I would look somewhere more lateral for this partner.

Otherwise, just about anyone you trust will work.

As we've discussed, thinking pairs can also be online or on the phone. Most thinking pairs that I know of are. But some people do pairs handily at their workplace in a quiet side room or meeting space. That is good because in person is always best, even for fifteen minutes. But once you have established a bit of practice together, virtual works.

So how would you start?

Nothing could be simpler in the whole world. At first it is not exactly easy because we are up against a million years of not doing this. But quickly we get good at it. It seems to be, after all, what we arrived in this life expecting. So it is in there somewhere, eager to be hailed.

First, decide who is first to think. Confirm that the thinking partner will get the thinker going with an opening question (more on that in a second), and that they will not speak again until the thinker says they are done. *Until the thinker says so.* No guessing.

Also, no telling. Fear of being quoted or talked about is another kind of interruption. It inhibits the thinker. Confidentiality, on the other hand, builds psychological safety and space. So it matters that both of you confirm ahead of time that whatever is said will be confidential forever unless the thinker agrees otherwise.

With that in place, you can set a timer. That act, too, increases safety and ease. Glancing at a watch is a disaster. Sustained attention is all. And a timer that goes off gently, like a Tibetan chime, works best. I know you will want to use your phone's clock app because it is right there in your hand/pocket/case/bloodstream. And it can work. But you have to be sure everything else is silenced. Everything. Notifications are death to the promise. This is obvious, but readily denied.

The first turn starts. The thinking partner asks this question (or one so nearly like it, it might as well be this one):

What do you want to think about, and what are your thoughts?

(Note the difference between that question and, say, 'What is your problem today?' Or 'How can I help you?' Or even 'What do you want to talk about?')

And that is an important point: the thinker does not have to talk.

They can, if they choose, be silent the entire time. Their job is to *think*. Often the most important insights arise in the thinker's silence, aided by the partner's silence. I hope you get to experience this.

The partner then keeps their eyes on the eyes of the thinker and does not look away for a second. They keep their face warm and interested. But not gooey. They stay interested in where the thinker will go *next*. They do not utter a string of 'uh-huh's. Their attention, and a once-in-a-century nod, will be doing the 'I'm listening'/'I understand'/'I'm interested' job of the 'uh-huh'. 'Uh-huh' interrupts, rushes and can even guide. Attention allows.

Of course, there will be the occasional teensy-phrase response from the partner. And I cannot describe that here. It is not predictable and will be needed only because the thinker said something funny, or shared a very, very, very happy thing, or disclosed a very, very, very sad thing, or asked something like, 'Am I making any sense?' The point is that on the one hand the partner does not introduce a single thing that could distract or detour or push, and on the other, they are not like an anvil or a dishwasher. They are alive and fully engaged. Communicating that aliveness takes very little but specific movement, mostly as understanding from the eyes.

Rarely, but now and then, during the five minutes, the thinker will ask the partner a question which, of course, the partner will answer, but so briefly as to rival the half-life of a particle.

Back to eyes for a moment. Not every culture interprets 'eyes-on-the-eyes-of-the-thinker' as respect and encouragement to keep going. For some cultures it is an insult. So you may have to negotiate this key behaviour. But remember that 'cultural' does not always equal 'good'. Some cultural taboos about eye contact, for example, are based on the assumption of inherent or positional superiority. So that may need negotiating just as much.

A perfect example of this cultural injunction about eyes is the messaging of male culture. As I have mentioned in other writing, this taboo may need to be addressed before male-to-male thinking pairs can work well. Some men tell me that if a man looks into the eyes of another man for longer than three seconds, it will be interpreted as either a request for sex or a threat of violence. That is sad,

I agree. And to women it is shocking. But if you are a man, it will probably be essential to raise this cultural issue with your potential thinking partner. I wish it weren't so, but apparently it is. Sustained attention in a thinking pair has only to do with generating thinking, not a thing to do with sex or violence. Quite, quite the opposite.

What's missing from this listening picture? Comments. Interjections. Questions. Wholesale hauling of the thinker to somewhere else. Agreement. Disagreement. Anything at all uninvited by the thinker.

What replaces that? A force of Nature: uninterruptive, generative attention. It is the force that produces consistent, courageous, ever-improving independent thinking. That kind of result cannot come from attention that squirms, getting ready to talk, preparing to be the expert. It cannot come from attention focused only on what has been said, and not on what is about to be thought.

This kind of attention, this rare kind of listening, as we know, is *different*. Thinking pairs are not conversations. They are not consulting or counselling or even coaching in its usual modes. Thinking pairs are a unique structure in which the human mind can venture forth with no shackles, no leash, no collapsing into the listener's lead. That is why they are so fruitful.

The promise changes our listening.

The timer pings. The thinker wraps up. You switch roles. You will probably feel a gentle exuding of recognition of the sparkling thing that has just happened. But as the listener it is best not to comment on the session. It is theirs, not yours. When the thinker's session is over, it's over.

And the next one begins.

That's what usually happens. Five uninterrupted minutes of self-respect and productivity. But occasionally, very occasionally, the thinker will stall. And if they *say* they are done, actually *say* so, the partner has to do something. There is still time in the turn, but the thinker has stopped. So how can the partner keep the thinker going without telling them what to think?

Great question. Huge question. The promise of no interruption changes the answer.

This juncture is dangerous. This is where the listener will be salivating to lob their by-now arguably awesome insights, knowledge and experience into the idling mind of the thinker. That will blow up everything. The point of the five minutes is to keep the thinker going *for themselves*. Not to turn their self into yourself. Nothing prepares us for this challenge. If the thinker does not need your brilliant insights to keep them going, what do they need?

They need a catalyst. That need can be met with a question. But not the one you might think. They need one that acknowledges this little-known finding: if the mind has generated waves of independent thought and then stops, it can almost certainly generate more. Not everybody knows that. Most people think that when someone stops thinking for a second, they are done. That's because no one ever checked. So you can check.

And this is the best way I know of to check. Ask the question that will generate more independent waves. I know of only one that does it magnificently:

What more do you think?

Yes. That simple. And that open. And that fit for purpose.

But doesn't it sound like you didn't hear the thinker say they were finished?

No, not if you both know what you are doing. The 'what more'? question acknowledges the finding that when there has been some thinking, there can be more. And I promise you, it will work. I came to it, as you know, slowly and with scepticism. But results are results, and no amount of counter-habit discomfort can justify ignoring them.

The question can be made even more potent if it allows for feelings and for the censored to be said (and, conversely, for the thinker to know that saying something is an option, not a requirement):

What more do you think, or feel, or want to say?

I have seen so much brilliance from that question, I now can hardly wait to ask it. If I believed in being a true believer, I would be one about this question. The human mind longs for this question. And when it receives it, it takes off.

So it's good to memorize it. You won't think you will forget it, but most people do. Or they botch it. How can you botch that simple sequence? You might well wonder. But I won't tell you in order not to put the botchings into your head. You can just memorize the question and avert the mess.

A tip: if you can't remember the question in full, you can shorten it to, 'What more do you think or feel?' And if that is too much to remember, you can go shorter with, 'What more do you think?' Or even shorter with, 'What more?' But not 'What?'

Also not so good is: 'What *else* do you think . . .?' 'What else' asks for difference. 'What more' allows for expansion.

Won't some other question do just as well? Maybe. But I have not found another that accomplishes this specific thing of generating more *independent* thinking when the thinker has stopped. If you find one, wake me in the night.

Another word about the counter-intuitive nature of repeating the question. The finding I mentioned – that if the thinker has generated more waves of thinking, they almost always can generate even more – was for me a mystery for a long time. But soon it became clear that the reason the repeated question worked was that it actually was not repeated. It was not the same question. The thinker registered it as a new question. It was the same words, but a different question.

I think that is because in each successive asking the context of the question is fresh, and so the thinker's mind hears the question as fresh. Isn't that wonderful? And knowing that makes it not only more comfortable to keep asking it until there is no more response to it, it makes it a pleasure.

Sometimes the 'what more' question produces a brand-new wave of thinking. It may also produce a solution that comes from 'nowhere'. It may generate an insight that changes the entire direction of the next couple of minutes. It can confirm earlier understandings. Or it can shatter them. Those results will feel comfortable to you as the partner because they hold recognizable value. And you will be impressed by how the promise of no interruption allowed those results to manifest in such a short time.

But occasionally you will not be impressed. You will ask the question and the thinker will say more or less what they just said. But *they* will be impressed. They will act as if it was the first time they had thought those things. This moment confused me for ages. I couldn't understand why their repetition could be so satisfying, even exciting, to the thinker. It made me wonder if this whole thing might be flawed.

But I began to notice that when I was the thinker, sometimes I did exactly that. I 'repeated' what I had just said. And it felt great. Something new had happened. I had progressed. So why?

I think that, as with the 'what more' question, it is because that kind of repetition is not repetition. It may be the same words, but it is not the same context. The thought now emerges from the new context which is the waves of thinking they just had. And so the thinker experiences the thought afresh, maybe even really sees the thought when before they just grazed it. In any number of ways the thinker's relation to the 'repeated' thought is different, even if on paper the thought itself isn't.

Sometimes this difference is not even substantive. Sometimes it is a shift internally that the listener cannot see, but the thinker can feel. Sometimes it is a new emotional relationship with the thought.

So I have become impressed by those thinker-'repetition' moments, now understanding that, yes, *it matters what the thinker says, but it matters more what happens for them because they say it.*

Isn't it just like the human mind not to squander a single second?

And finishing?

At the end of the second five minutes, the thinking pair is nearly over. How then do you 'end' it? I agree you can't just say 'great' and pick up your things. So what might keep you both thinking well between thinking pairs and even add another catalyst for your best thinking throughout the day?

Appreciation. But not as we usually understand it. Appreciation at the end of a thinking pair is not a thank-you-for-your-service thing. It is far bigger than that. It is a recognition of a quality in a person. Now I know you were probably told not to do this. We all were, one way or another. We might get a 'big head'. (What is that?) Or become 'too big for our boots'. (Boots?) Or grow conceited. That stuff sticks. So we need to replace it with a better take on reality. Also, we probably need to know that conceit and all of those 'too big' things come from too little appreciation in life, not too much.

What is true is that we humans need to hear good things about ourselves. And we need to say them to others. We both gain. We gain ease and confidence, and we envy less. And so we think better. Depriving each other of appreciation in the name of some imagined immodesty is a kind of neglect. So we need to experience appreciation often. A thinking pair is one place we can do that every day.

Try it at the end of the pair. As a daily practice it in itself keeps us thinking for ourselves. It opens up the day. And our hearts. It gives us courage. We remember it in tough moments. It develops us.

For this to work, though, the appreciation has to be very, very short. People cannot hear much appreciation without getting woozy. Again, it is too counter-upbringing. Guilt sets in before we count to one.

Also, the best appreciation is about a quality in the person that is not based on the content of the person's thinking turn. It needs to be a quality you've noticed in them generally.

And it needs to be free of any mention of the dynamics of the session like: 'Your listening so well made such a huge difference to me,' or 'Your thinking was marvellous.' Appreciations like that can register subtly as assessments. They can weaken the safety for the next time. This is not a performance review. It is a stepping back from the moment and a bringing to mind this whole person and their whole life as you know it. Qualities that are who they *are* will be what they internalize and use, far beyond the thinking time with you.

Okay, you may say, *but if we are having a thinking pair every day, we'll eventually run out of things to appreciate about each other.* Maybe.

So you can just 'start over'. We can fruitfully hear the same positive thing about ourselves. In fact, we will most likely have forgotten it anyway, such is the anti-gravity of appreciation. But the odds are you won't run out of things to say. My weekly thinking partner and I have been appreciating each other every week for eleven years. That's 528 appreciations. And we haven't started over yet.

You really would not believe how hard appreciation is for people. Some people say it is the most challenging of all the thinking environment components. Early indoctrination is a despot.

But it is worth defying. I agree with Carl Rogers who asserted that the human baby arrives complete with unconditional self-regard and expects to find that as the culture of their life. Children have to be cudgelled into giving up this expectation. We grow unwillingly into adults who disdain and withhold appreciation. Fortunately, thinking pairs can restore both our experience of it and our expertise at it. And before we know it, we live it.

That is reason enough to do it. But what matters most about appreciation is that demonstrably it helps us think for ourselves well.

How's that for an endorsement from Nature?

Let's go back to the beginning. The one just after we hear those words: 'What do you want to think about, and what are your thoughts?' That moment. I hope very much that you will have that moment every day. Regardless of where your thinking goes in those five minutes, that very first moment is worth the whole investment. Just to be in the presence of that question with the promise intact changes things.

The question and the promise merge, and something happens. You hold that something close; you let it in; you let it let you breathe. You cherish it. It is different from any other moment in your life. The moment after the question. The promise of no interruption has changed that moment forever.

For years I could not – I still cannot – find words to describe this nearly hallowed moment. But my colleague Maryse Barak has. She says it this way:

That moment just after the opening question is: an experience of *no fear*, a territory of *possibility*, a guarantee of *no agenda* whatsoever, a *terrain created by both, owned by one.*

Yes. That is it.

I am sure such a beautiful experience would be part of a life lived from birth to death in a thinking environment.

So might you set up a thinking pair? If so, you almost certainly will find that this daily practice frees you, dignifies you, lets your mind do what it was meant to do and your life be what it was meant to be.

That wondrous first moment and the thinking that follows honour our humanity. They let us live for a tiny time in this promise-imbued world so that the interruptive world all around us is easier to navigate, is no longer the rack it was.

Thinking pairs let us understand the promise in our bones.

Five minutes. That's all it takes to change a day.

Even a life.

35. The Thinking Session

And if there were more time? If we wanted to make even more progress on an issue, big or small, to free ourselves definitively from blocks, for example, or to change a feeling for good, or to understand why we do or feel something or why we don't; if we wanted to figure out our vision and start that journey; if we wanted to gain courage; if we wanted to come to terms with something once and for all; if we wanted to take stock thoroughly of our successes or our challenges, or to figure out whether something is true – what would we do?

We would think about it under the conditions of a thinking pair, but for longer and usually, therefore, more deeply. We might call it a thinking session. As with thinking pairs we would be in the presence of the promise of no interruption and oceans of generative attention and the widest possible welcome to do our own thinking.

And to be sure nothing sabotaged it, we would, as with the thinking pair, set aside a discrete, boundaried time for it. Some like an hour or more, thirty minutes for each person. I do, too. Usually they aim for once a week. But you'll find your favourite.

We would use the longer time to go as far as we possibly can with our own thinking, spurred by the generative attention of our thinking partner and, when needed, the 'What more . . .?' question. And because a thinking session is throughout an act of dismantling denial and of establishing psychological safety, we would, most of the time, phenomenally, break through all of our own blocks, sometimes so gracefully neither of us would see the breakthrough process at work. And we would go all the way to the ambitious outcome we hoped for.

But if we did get stuck, and 'What more . . .?' could not produce more thinking, and yet we still had more time and wanted more results, our partner and we would know just how to find and get rid of the block that had stopped us, so that our thinking would take off again. And it would.

The lived promise not to interrupt, I think, leads naturally to a thinking session. The promise in that way changes the way we develop ourselves, and the way we pursue and resolve our big issues. It changes how we progress our lives.

If people lived in a thinking environment from birth to death, I can imagine that a thinking session, or something very close to it, would be a taken-for-granted, but prized part of their week, not to be missed.

Even in our current shatteringly interruptive world I have seen this high-results outcome thousands of times. The thinking session is a bountiful resource, a spring.

So I propose that here for a little while we consider the thinking session in some detail. We will be able to see the impact of the promise of no interruption and the impact of a thinking environment on the human mind engaged in its most consequential work.

If you already have thinking sessions in your life, you will know how exquisitely the session allows the mind to unfold. And now you will see the thinking session at its most elegant, because we have discovered new things about how the mind seems to find its own questions. We have proposed beautiful changes in the ways the thinking partner thinks their way to the next question when needed. You will see that these new findings suggest just why the promise works and how much of life it changes.

If you are new to this, maybe when you finish this book you will invite someone to be a thinking session partner with you. If you do, you will in the future reflect, I predict, on this juncture in your life with a smile and a private nod to the results.

36. Recognition Not Creation

Before we get started properly on this exploration, I think it is important to consider this. The thinking session process looks for all the world like a creation, a methodology, a model, a framework, a thing. I am forever fighting those descriptors. They imply a conscious concoction.

The thinking session process is anything but. It is a recognition. It is an ongoing outcome of noticing over the years what the human mind seems to do to get on an independent thinking roll and to stay there.

We've seen a lot, and we continue to watch, to notice, to see more. What we call a 'thinking session' is not a methodology because it is never finished. If it is anything, it is a kind of life form. Nature is too complex for us to penetrate fully or entirely accurately. So we cannot complete it. We can only keep our eyes open.

So we do. And what we observe is that the human mind wants to, and will, given half a chance, think fully for itself until it can't. Then it either wants input of some kind or to find and remove blocks that have emerged. It wants to gain force again and build.

Crucially, we observe that thinking blocks are almost always untrue assumptions lived as true. And we have observed how the mind seems to deal with those assumptions, to find them and remove them fast when it can. It is fascinating.

So here we will explore just how it seems to do that: what exactly it seems to do to gather energy, and what it does when it stops so that it can start again.

The reason it is important to know what a person's mind seems to do to keep going is that when it can't, it will need our help as the listener, as the thinking partner. It will need us to do for it what it had been doing for itself. Why under these optimal conditions it, nevertheless, stops, I don't know yet. But when it does, it needs us to simulate what it had been doing. So we need to know something about what that is. In those few but critical moments, we need to be sharp, knowledgeable and entirely alert to what has just happened.

First, then, we need a handful of off-the-chart beautiful findings about independent thinking, some of which we have touched on. They are marvels, and a thrill to notice, to contemplate, to scrutinize, to learn, to use and always to doubt. From doubting comes discovery. Doubting is a thinker's best friend. Paradoxically, doubting produces confidence. Every single one of these 'findings' has come from the harmony of doubt and confidence.

It is exactly this built-in cluster of findings that, when consciously understood and elegantly practised, develops us into increasingly sharp independent thinkers and invaluable thinking partners for each other.

So let's look at these findings. There are not many, but they are gold.

37. Findings

You already know these. Like incisive questions, you have done them
all of your life. I surmise they are straight from DNA land. Any
chance you could – between interruptions, after interruptions, head-
ing off the next interruption – you've done them. We all have. It's
what we do. Someone listens, and we do these things. We were made
for this, this relationship between the human mind and the complex
force that is generative attention. It is a love affair. It is our destiny.

But we don't know that we know these things. We don't see ourselves doing them. We just do them, and carry on.

This means that all of these findings are already in us. They are
right there ready to be realized. We know how our mind stays on
an independent thinking roll. We know how it breaks through
blocks. We know how it finds the information it needs, figures out
why it feels and does things, engages with assumptions, and how it
leaps over debris to a new life.

In that sense then these findings are autonomic. We know them
a bit the way we know how to produce heartbeats and pancreatic
juices and skin. We don't know that we know how, but clearly we
do, because we do them. We can see the evidence in the fact that
we are alive. It is the same with the inner workings of independent
thinking. Because we do it, we must know how. But we don't know
that we know. So we have to dissect it and look.

Similarly, because inherently we know how we think for ourselves, we also know how to help someone else think for
themselves, too, if they pause and can't start again spontaneously.
We've known it all along. We just haven't known that we knew.

Now we do.

Most of these findings we have already explored here. The ten components of a thinking environment, for example, is a whole system

of findings. We also have seen the power of repeating a question. And we know about the importance of using the thinker's own words if we refer to their thinking. People think in their own specific words, not just in their own language.

We also have seen how vital easeful, engaged silence is in producing independent thinking.

And we have noted the psychological-safety-making dimension of our agreement to be wholly confidential with what we hear from each other.

All of those findings work together to produce independent thinking.

Here are five more we have not yet considered. The first one is the new one. It is, I think, astonishingly beautiful.

Waves, Pauses, Considerations

Enchantingly, the human mind seems to think in waves and pauses. After a wave of thought there seems to be a pause. Inside the pause something almost Delphic happens that produces another wave.

So to understand how to generate a new wave of thinking in someone else when they can't do it for themselves, all we have to do is understand what goes on in the pause between waves.

We think that the intriguing process inside the pause is a series of (most likely five) considerations. The mind seems to use these considerations to find the perfect breakthrough question to ask itself so that it can produce a new wave of thinking.

The mind seems to consider:

Whether or not it still wants to think for itself
What it has just done (in 'process' terms such as: generate
    more waves, set a new thinking outcome, find
    assumptions, identify a key assumption, determine
    whether that assumption is true, find a true liberating one,
    embed it, etc.)
Whether its desired thinking outcome has changed

What it needs now in order to reach that outcome

What question will meet that need

So all we need to do as the thinking partner is to understand these considerations and reason our way through them to the perfect question. That turns out to be simple (in that 'other side of complexity' sense), logical and, before you know it, fun.

We are finding freshly good results from this development in the practice of thinking sessions because we now use reason, rather than a 'parts and map' memorizing of questions and routes, to determine the next question for the thinker.

Most impressively, it is looking as if those silent considerations as a road to the next question have equipped the thinking partner as nothing else ever has. So we will look in detail at these few, powerful considerations in action in a moment.

First, I just want to clarify that the pauses between waves are not just the ones we as the listener/partner can detect. These fructuous pauses are happening right along, but most of them are too fast to notice. We can, however, spot evidence of them in the shift in thinking that the mind just did. That spontaneous, fresh thinking must have come from something that happened in the pause. Examining that shift in thinking, we can hypothesize what the thinker seems to have done in the pause to produce it. We can 'notice' those considerations in there.

The crucial-for-us-as-listener pause, though, is the one we can actually experience. It is the 'I'm finished' pause when the thinker says they are done for the moment because they are no longer generating ideas. That is when as the partner we need to have this emerging knowledge of what the human mind does in a pause to produce new waves. That is, we need to know these considerations and go through them in a flash in our own minds to find the next question. In that way we are simulating the thinker's own process.

So you could say that learning how to be a good thinking partner means learning everything we can about those considerations that go on spontaneously in the pauses between waves.

Rosemary Clark, owner of Think Big in South Africa, proposes the following as the milieu for these considerations. She thinks of the pauses as the thinker's time of listening. She wrote to me:

> I have been thinking about the question: 'What is actually going on in the pauses?' I realize that when we pause, we are actually *listening*. We are listening first to our own bodies, i.e. to the authenticity of what we are saying to ourselves.
>
> We are listening also to our partner's response, what their bodies, eyes, being, are saying back to us. And we are extending our listening out into the 'ether', to the wisdom that resides there and that supports and holds us in our thinking, the wisdom of the ages, of the elders, of all the thinking that has gone before us.
>
> We also are checking for safety. Safety and trust are paramount to our being able to think for ourselves.
>
> There is a lot of work going on in the pause. It is not a 'dead' space.
>
> This thought makes me realize just what is available to us when we are allowed really to think for ourselves.

I agree.

And I think that this 'listening' that Rosemary recognizes allows the thinker to navigate the considerations spontaneously, speedily and with grace.

When we do a session together in a moment, I hope, if you have been familiar with the former way of learning the thinking session, you will see how this new 'waves/pauses/considerations' understanding is simply leagues more elegant than the 'parts and map' construct. It is also so much simpler.

But, of course, elegance and simplicity adore each other.

Innate Breakthrough Questions

The breakthrough questions, the ones the mind uses to start a fresh wave of thinking, seem to be from a cluster of what we might call 'innate' questions. I say 'innate' because these questions seem to be variously but predictably the tool for breaking an impasse in human thinking. When you note those breakthrough moments, you can usually glimpse one or more of these questions at work each time.

These are the familiar session questions demonstrated in my other two books. But the arriving at them, as I have said, is different and easier now. We came up with those breakthrough questions in the first place because we could 'see' their 'footprints' in the mind's suddenly unstuck, new thinking. As with the considerations in the pause, we deconstructed the thinker's new thinking to find those questions as the road to those insights.

The promise of no interruption makes room for those questions as interruption simply cannot. In that way the promise changes and restores even how the mind itself can work.

Interest or Curiosity?

This may not seem important. But the more I think about it, the more salience I think it has. You often hear that to listen well we have to be curious. I disagree. I think we need to be curious in all sorts of ways in life. Curiosity is vital to human progress. But when we are listening to ignite people's thinking, we need to lay aside curiosity and replace it with interest. They are fascinatingly different things. Curiosity is subtly self-focused. Interest is subtly other-focused. So as we listen, curiosity can be curtailing. Interest is freeing.

Thirty-five Per Cent

How often does the thinker come to a dead-end impasse and need the partner to generate and ask the next question? How often does the thinker need the partner to simulate the process the thinker was progressing until that moment? About 35 per cent of the time, according to Monica Schüldt's survey.

Sixty-five per cent of the time the thinker's mind does all of that 'considerations' work itself and comes up with the question, asks it of itself and vrooms. The promise makes all of that happen spontaneously, organically. So two-thirds of all thinking sessions will get to the splendid, productive outcomes the thinker wants from the session while the partner gives uncorrupted, generative attention; and only occasionally, because only when the thinker says they are finished for the moment, does the partner ask, 'What more . . .?' This efficiency of the human mind's use of attention is, I think, one of the natural wonders of the world.

Equally, at any given second in a session the thinker can get stuck, and 'What more . . .?' won't work any more. So our expertise in navigating this 35 per cent eventuality is practically a moral imperative.

Blocks

We are finding that these things can block thinking:

Missing components of a thinking environment
Physical distractions
Missing, partial or poor information
Unreleased feelings
Untrue assumptions lived as true

Our minds seem to scan for these when they are stuck. If we are in a thinking environment, the first four are probably not an issue. A thinking environment would have prevented them. For that matter, a thinking environment will have spontaneously identified and dispatched most untrue assumptions in our way as well.

But when an assumption won't budge by itself, we need to know these findings about blocks, to help it:

Assumptions

The key block to thinking is an untrue assumption, lived as true.
The key liberator of thinking is a true liberating assumption.

An assumption is often the answer to *why* we do or feel something.

The criteria for assessing the truth or untruth of an assumption are:

Information (is the assumption factually provable?)
Logic (is the assumption logically provable?)

Those findings about assumptions look pedestrian in a list like that. In an experience of them, however, they are celestial.

The problem here is the word 'assumption'. It is so, so boring. It sits there, lumpy, completely not singing. But off the page and into experience it is just the most, most lyrical, full-throated thing you can imagine. We do and feel and build and destroy and conceive practically everything in our lives on the basis of assumptions. They star. And to see them for what they are, to see the scope of their impact, is electrifying.

Assumptions have their most severe impact as the key blocks to human thinking. Untrue assumptions lived as true are what block us nearly always. And so we can bypass the usual question about blocks ('What is stopping you?') and head right for the key block by asking:

What might you be assuming that is stopping you?

That question streamlines the other into a laser of insight. Hearing it and absorbing it, the thinker suddenly grasps formerly occluded roots of immobility. It is that accurate and direct. 'What is stopping you?', on the other hand, is mostly a sloppy, round-the-houses and time-consuming version of 'What are you assuming that is stopping you?'

There is a sense in which, at its best, most counselling, most therapy, most coaching is an interface with the untrue limiting assumptions that we live as true, and that are the cause of our neuroses, our malaise, our fears, our stagnation, our self-loathing, our functional stupidity. Assumptions. The direct cause. And the direct route to the sky. Don't you wish someone had told you that when you were eight?

We'll see this at work in a little while when we simulate a

thinking session here. But my fondest hope is that you will find a real live thinking partner and experience this in the flesh for yourself.

Best of all I hope you will get very, very good at it. Life begins to have more time, intelligent play, dependable rigour, realizable dreams, frequent smiles and exuberance with which to sojourn and paint the world when we become masters of our assumptions. Taking our *own* brushes in hand, placing *our* new canvas under the perfect tree, we look. We see. Life starts to happen differently.

There are all kinds of knowledge in the world that change life. But in my view the knowledge of the starring role of assumptions is tops. Hands down.

These findings are elegant gleanings from observing in action the independent thinking of people. They challenge most of the 'helping' norms of our society, quietly, surely. They express the power of the promise of no interruption. And they reveal the 'inside story' of the components of a thinking environment.

They are not static. They are stunning.

What's Left

There are two more ever-appearing findings, though they are uber-geeky (deliciously so). But I am finding, as I mentioned (and as humans have known for millennia), that experience produces the deepest learning.

So I propose we 'do' a thinking session here so that you can 'experience' it. I know this is not optimal. Ideally, we would be in person and you would be the thinker first. Paradoxically it is through being the thinker that we learn how to be the thinking partner.

And then we would switch roles, and you would be my partner while I think. That would truly be a useful first experience of a thinking session and of all these findings in action. We would then do another one and another one. And only then would we look at the on-paper material about it, if then.

But this is a book, and that is that. Even so, shall we see how much we can glean from imagining a session in which you are the partner and a pretend colleague is the thinker? I will cover as many of the eventualities as workable so that you will be challenged at as many junctures as possible, seeing as many of the findings at work as possible.

And then we can talk about it all.

This will be good.

But first, just a couple of things to get it going.

38. Preparing For It

The Desire

First, we need the desire. This cannot be said too many times: we need to want like anything to think for ourselves. We need to want to think for ourselves more than we want another person to think for us. Most people are so used to surrendering to other people's thinking they've lost the courage to generate their own, and even think they *cannot* produce any better thinking than they already have, and certainly not better than someone else's.

But we can rejoice in this: whatever thinking we have done under interruptive conditions is not the thinking we will do under uninterruptive ones. The promise of no interruption changes the thinking itself. Thinking gets better. It is more imaginative. It is more adventurous, responsible, more 'no kidding?', more useful. Knowing this, we find it easy to invoke the desire to think for ourselves. In fact, the desire becomes irrepressible.

The Singular Purpose

Next, we need to keep in mind the *singular* purpose of a thinking session: to *generate one person's independent thinking as far as possible in the time agreed.*

That is a radical and endgame-changing purpose.

And it stays the same throughout. If this singular purpose changes, what we are doing is no longer a thinking session. It is something else. That means we now do different things. So we need to note regularly that the singular purpose of the thinker's independent thinking is still intact in both the thinker and the partner. (This seems to be the first consideration in each pause.)

This singular purpose and the promise are symbiotic. They practically *are* each other.

Wondering

This purpose/promise duo changes things. It changes even *what we wonder about* when we listen. Have you ever wondered about what you wonder about when you are listening? I think that is an interesting question. What *do* you wonder about when you are listening?

It depends, of course, on the purpose of the listening. And in a thinking session the singular purpose of producing independent thinking stops us from wondering how we can come in with those beating-on-the-door insights we have been muzzling. It stops us from wondering about what question we could ask that would make the thinker tweet about the genius they were just with.

The purpose and promise keep us wondering instead about how far the thinker might be able to go in their own thinking before they need ours. We need to wonder about that so hard, so feverishly, so euphorically, we wouldn't dream of wondering about how we could plop down and plump the thinker's cushions just so.

So the 'culture setting' question in our minds as we listen needs to be:

How far can the thinker go in their own thinking before they need mine?

And when they get there, and they say they are finished, we need to wonder this:

How much further even than that can they go for themselves?

In fact, the thinker also needs to *wonder* that. It is the singular purpose of the session, to generate their fullest possible independent thinking in the time agreed.

Way of Being

Also, if I am your partner, I will have to *be* a certain way consistently. I will have to *be* a thinking environment. That means, of course, that I will have to embody the ten behaviours we've talked about, the ten components of a thinking environment. I also will need to:

- *Know* that you can think for yourself better than I can think *for* you
- Keep my eyes on your eyes
- Keep my expression warm and engaged, expressive of *being with* you without leading you, resonating with (but not mirroring) your changes in mood and meaning
- Regard you as my thinking peer regardless of any status or power differential
- Be at ease inside
- Encourage you silently: championing, not competing with, you
- Notice what I respect about you
- Focus on your vast capacity for good
- Welcome your feelings
- Enjoy the ways we are different from each other
- Enjoy, too, the ways we are just like each other
- Speak only when you invite me to

If I do all of these things, plus embody the ten components, you may have thought many times in a non-thinking environment, sometimes for many months (years even) about something, and under these conditions of the promise, swiftly break through recalcitrant blocks (usually untrue assumptions), come to a formerly inaccessible understanding, find a bespoke way forward and even grow compassion, determination, energy and serenity.

Being a Thinking Environment can produce all of that.

39. Just Before

As we begin a prototype thinking session here together, note again that each next question is determined not from a 'script', not as preset choreography, not from linear, decontextualized inevitabilities. We determine the next question by *thinking through* the considerations.

The findings do not dictate. They inform.

This is especially true of 'innate questions'. The 'innate questions' are a precise but supple natural force. However, when recited, they look (on paper) and sound as if they are linear, sequential, even formulaic; but they are not at all. They can occur in any order, any time. They can unfold, enfold, flop, flip, stride, tiptoe, double back or never look back. Anything.

They can appear suddenly or curl their way into and out of a partial sequence of thought at any second. They are needed only when they are needed; and the thinker's mind pauses and engages in those considerations: where it is, what it wants to accomplish next, what it needs to get there and what question, if appropriate, will meet that need. Wherever and whenever.

40. Doing It

Now let's start.

Let's say you and a colleague meet. You agree that she will be the thinker; you will be the thinking partner. You set a gentle timer. Your eyes meet. You ask:

What do you want to think about, and what are your thoughts?

She savours the question. Eventually she speaks.

I want to think about tension. Mine.

She is quiet. For nearly a minute she says nothing. Neither do you.

She talks for a while. You are intrigued. You have ideas for her. You keep them to yourself. You return, as if to a mantra, to her, to where she will go next with her thoughts. You remember to wonder how far she can go with her thinking before she needs yours.

She is quiet again. She pulls out a notebook and writes something down. You don't ask what. You don't look at the paper. You keep your eyes on her eyes, wherever they go.

She looks out the window. She smiles. You wonder what she is seeing, out there, in there. You say nothing. You make sure your face is soft, your eyes still, warm, unwaveringly with her.

She talks some more. You realize you could never have predicted that insight. You are glad you didn't speak. What she just said answered a question more challenging, richer, than the one you had in mind for her.

That's all, she says.

You remember she means that it is all she can think of for the moment. You remember to wonder how much further than that she can go. You remember the finding that if there have been waves of thinking, there can be more.

You run through the considerations in your mind:

Yes, we are both still committed to her independent thinking.

What she has just done is complete all the waves of thinking she can for now.

Her session outcome is still to think about her tension.

Given that, and the findings, what she needs is again to generate more waves.

The question that will serve that need is:

What more do you think, or feel, or want to say?

She looks away. She is quiet for a little longer. She speaks again. She stiffens. She cries a bit. She smiles. She tells you her thought. You nod gently. Your eyes stay warm. She talks again. She realizes an error in her thinking. You marvel.

That's all, she says.

You smile. You shift in your seat a bit, look back into her eyes, go like the wind through the considerations, noting the progress through them to be exactly as before. You wonder if she will baulk at being asked again the very same question. Then you remember the finding that this repeated question is not registered as the same question, because the context has changed. You relax. You ask, gently, slowly:

And what more do you think, or feel, or want to say?

She speaks. For nearly fifteen minutes she alternately talks and is quiet. In every quiet time she says nothing about being finished. You know she is still thinking. You keep your attention alive. After a while she seems to come to a conclusion. She has resolved something. She is quiet again. But you remember that until she says that she is finished, she is not.

A few minutes later she is. She says so.

And you again go through the considerations in your mind, so fast no one would notice:

We are both still committed to her independent thinking.

She has just completed all the waves of thinking she can for now.

She hasn't changed her session outcome: to think about her tension.

Given that, and the findings, what she needs is to generate more waves.

The question that will serve that need is still:

What more do you think, or feel, or want to say?

She looks into your eyes and starts to speak. She keeps her eyes on yours and is silent. This is the longest anyone has ever held your gaze without speaking. It is a challenge not to break the connection. You resume conscious interest in where she will go next, even not knowing where she is. You relax your face. You trust her as a thinker. You trust that your attention will keep her going as long and as far as she can go.

And she goes far. She covers ground you could never have thought of. She has insights you had, but many you didn't. You learn even as you attend. She muses in silence. You are starting to feel comfortable in her quiet times. You can see the results.

She stops. She looks at you again. She speaks.

I think I am completely done now.

You nod and quickly go through the considerations in your mind again:

Yes, we are both still committed to her independent thinking.

What she has just done is *say* she is completely finished, but there were more waves after I asked the question. So we don't know for sure that she is finished.

Her session outcome, to think about her tension, is still the same as far as she has indicated.

Given that, and the findings, her need now is to generate even more thinking if she can.

And the question that will serve that need is again:

What more do you think, or feel, or want to say?

To your amazement she takes off again, thinking, talking, pausing, tearing, writing down something else. There is new energy in what she is doing. She even laughs, and you join her. You both smile. Then she says definitively:

I really am completely done now.

With new confidence you do just as you did a few minutes ago because she did have waves from the 'What more?' question even after saying she was finished completely. But you add a bit to acknowledge what just happened.

Just to be sure, given that you did generate more waves just now, what more do you think, or feel, or want to say?

No, I am really done this time.

The considerations again:

Yes, we are both still committed to her independent thinking.

What she has just done is produce no more waves from the 'what more?' question.

Her session outcome may still be the same: to think about her tension; but we don't know for sure now, given that she had no more thoughts. She may feel she has accomplished the outcome. We don't know.

Given that, and the findings, what she needs is now different. It logically has to be to determine what she wants to accomplish further, if anything, in the session.

The question that will meet that need is:

We still have some time. What more, if anything, would you like to accomplish with the rest of our session?

She lets that in. She looks back at her notes. She looks away. She stays quiet. Then she speaks.

I want to know how to become a person who is relaxed and not worried at the drop of a hat, or on guard all of the time. Yes, that's what I want. All of that.

You remember the finding about memorizing her exact words, if you possibly can. You know you can't. It is too long. So what can you do here?

You know that you cannot guess how *she* would shorten it or paraphrase it without ripping her out of her personal culture and boring her with your anaemic version of her vibrant construction. So you reason out the next (and obvious) question:

Can you possibly put that in fewer words, still holding all of the meaning, so that I can memorize it?

She does.

I want to become a relaxed person.

Good. You memorize that.

Now what? How do you help her think for herself towards this new session outcome? How do you help her to 'become a relaxed person'?

Well, that's worth a few moments here because this juncture is just about the most dangerous in the session. It is here that most people abandon the thinker's independence, subvert the singular purpose and take over. It is here that our habits of thinking for people scream so loud, having been starved during the session so far for so long, they silence all the newly absorbed findings. This is the moment when the thinking partner can turn into an ordinary think-for listener. And when they do, the thinker loses both dignity as a thinker and success beyond our imagining. So you teeter, feeling the gravity of your past.

You remember to go through the considerations. They are your friend. They will lead you logically to a perfect next question:

Yes, we are both still committed to her independent thinking.

What she has just done is determine a further outcome for the session.

Her session outcome has changed. It is now to 'become a relaxed person'.

(You think about what the findings would say about this outcome in this context. You see that her new outcome has come out of her first topic. It is not a new topic. But attention and 'what more?' did not accomplish this particular piece for her, i.e. they did not free her to 'become a relaxed person'. So it must be that she has run into a block. A block must have been what stopped her thinking. And to get rid of the block we have first to find it. You also remember the finding that the key block to thinking is usually an untrue assumption lived as true.)

What she needs then, given this new outcome and those findings, is to start the journey to find the block, an untrue limiting assumption.

The question that will serve that need is:

What might you be assuming that is stopping you from becoming a relaxed person?

It registers. You smile inside.

She comes up with three assumptions. She talks about them. She walks around them and wonders about them and remembers things that probably led to them. She thinks. You stay interested in where she will go next, knowing that at any second she could break through and accomplish her outcome. You wish she would come up with more assumptions. But you remember that always the point of the question is to get thinking, not answers. You relax.

That's all, she says.

You go again to the considerations:

We are both still committed to her independent thinking.

What she has just done is find some assumptions.

Her session outcome is still to become a relaxed person.

You consult the findings. The relevant one here is that if there have been some assumptions, there can be more.

Given that, and the findings, what she needs is to see if she can find more assumptions.

The question that will serve that need is:

What else might you be assuming that is stopping you from becoming a relaxed person?

You are pleased to have asked 'what else', not 'what more', because this time the search is only for different assumptions, not for expansion of the found ones.

She thinks of another one. And another. She thinks about them. She stops.

That's all.

Again the considerations, the same as a few minutes ago:

The commitment is the same.

What she has just done is the same.

Her session outcome has not changed.

So the need is the same. The next question, also, is:

What else might you be assuming that is stopping you from becoming a relaxed person?

She looks away.

No. I can't think of any more.

Now what? What can you do with all those assumptions? You remember that the human mind cannot deal with all of its assumptions at once and so she must find the key one, the one that is most blocking her. How can you know what that key assumption is? And given the finding that the key assumption is not key unless it is also *untrue*, how do you choose one and assess it?

You don't. She does. But can she do it herself? Wouldn't it be kind, not to mention clever, for you to jump in and do that for her? You are certain what the key untrue one is, having listened like a band of angels for so long. But it really is up to her, so what question will help her do it?

You are glad for the considerations:

We are both still committed to her independent thinking.

She has just found all of the limiting assumptions she can.

Her session outcome is still to become a relaxed person.

Given that, and the findings about assumptions, what she needs now is to identify the assumption she thinks is most stopping her. (It might be one she has said; but it might be a new one.)

The question that will serve that need is:

What are you assuming that is most stopping you from becoming a relaxed person?

She smiles. She knows. She says. But it is not one she had mentioned before.

I am assuming that some people might think I am not as dynamic as I was.

You know immediately, of course, that that assumption is possibly true. Some people certainly could think she is not as dynamic as she was, given the world's tension-saturated definition of 'dynamic' these days.

But you don't say all of that. You know she must think it through for herself and determine, given the criteria of facts and logic, whether it is true before you examine it together. Also, she might convince you otherwise – unlikely in this case but you never know. So you want to stay open to her argument while also staying true to the criteria of logic and information. A balancing act if there ever was one.

The considerations help, again:

We are both still committed to her independent thinking.

What she has just done is choose a key assumption.

Her session outcome is still to become a relaxed person.

Given that, and the findings, what she needs is to determine whether her key assumption is untrue.

The question that will serve that need is:

Do you think it is true that some people might think you are not as dynamic as you were?

She barely draws breath.

Yes, of course it is true. Lots of people think you have to be wired to be dynamic.

She thinks that through for a minute, and then confirms.

Yes, it is possibly true. Some people might think that.

Now what? You want to keep her thinking for herself. But you ponder this juncture of her having chosen a key assumption that is true. You know that she has not, therefore, found the actual key assumption because the actual key assumption has to be untrue. So she still has to find that.

What can you do to help her find, *for herself,* the key (untrue) assumption? You are stumped.

Join the club. This juncture has tripped up listeners forever. It is often at this point that a listener weakens and just asks a fantasy question like: 'Okay, but maybe they wouldn't think you are not as dynamic as you were. Imagine that for a minute. What would you do in that case to become a relaxed person?'

Yuck, you think. And I agree. There is nothing quite so unuseful as a fantasy scenario. It sometimes produces a couple of ideas, but they die on the way home.

What, then, you wonder, do the findings say about this situation when the thinker's chosen assumption is true?

Lots. And it is bewitching.

There are quite a few things I am grateful to have lived long enough to see. One of them is the question that finds the untrue assumption when the thinker's chosen one is true.

It turns out that it is hiding inside. An untrue assumption hides inside a true one. I think that is unsurpassingly cool to know. Let it in: an untrue assumption hides inside a true one. A take-home point if ever there was one.

And not only that, the untrue one actually has a relationship with the true one. It *causes* the true one to stop us. So it is not just some random untrue assumption hiding in the true one. It is an untrue one that *causes* the true one to stop us.

Knowing those two things: 1) that there is an untrue assumption hiding inside the true one, and 2) that the untrue one *causes* the true one to stop us, we can work out what the question is that will reveal it. The question will have to contain this causal relationship between the untrue assumption and the true one. So the question is likely to be this:

It is true that some people might think you are not as dynamic as you were. What are you assuming that causes that to stop you from becoming a relaxed person?

Isn't that a work of art? It took us ages to see it, but it was worth every error and dashed hope along the way.

Logging that finding, you go through the considerations to be sure:

We are both still committed to her independent thinking.

What she has just done is to confirm that her chosen key assumption is true.

Her session outcome is still to become a relaxed person.

Given that, and the findings about key assumptions, what she needs is to find the untrue assumption inside the true one.

The question that will serve that need is:

It is true that some people might think you are not as dynamic as you were. What are you assuming that causes that to stop you from becoming a relaxed person?

You ask it.

She frowns.

What? she asks.

You remind her about an untrue assumption hiding inside a true one, and its causal relationship with it. She nods. She asks you to ask it again. You do.

It is true that some people might think you are not as dynamic as you were. What are you assuming that causes that to stop you from becoming a relaxed person?

She lets it in. She looks up.

I am assuming that what people think of me matters more than what I think.

And that assumption, you reason, is untrue. The criteria of information and logic would say so. We're there!

But you know that if at all possible she has to see it as untrue, too. You cannot do that for her. And anyway, she may harness an argument you haven't thought of that makes the assumption possibly true. Staying open to that is important. So how do you engage her in determining for herself the truth or not of that assumption?

You've done this before, you realize, but in your mind you quickly go through the considerations to be sure:

We are both still committed to her independent thinking.

What she has just done is find the untrue assumption that is hiding in her first (true) chosen assumption.

Her session outcome is still to become a relaxed person.

Given that, and the findings about key assumptions, what she needs is to determine whether that new assumption is true or untrue.

The question that will serve that need is:

Do you think it is true that what people think of you is more important than what you think?

She knows immediately.

No. I do feel that sometimes. I like for people to think well of me and to look up to me a bit, to consider me a compelling person. But no, it is not true that what they think of me is more important than what I think.

Great, you think. We can go with this as the key limiting assumption. There is a God.

But now? You know she can't just go home with that insight. It is powerful, you can tell. But it does not get her to her desired session outcome, to know how to become a relaxed person. It is still only a lantern. You remember the finding that says that it is a true liberating assumption that takes us to our desired outcomes.

So the considerations:

We are both still committed to her independent thinking.

What she has just done is determine that the assumption hiding inside the true one is untrue. Therefore, she has just found the assumption blocking her.

Her session outcome is still to become a relaxed person.

Given that, and the findings about assumptions, what she needs is to find a true liberating assumption to replace the untrue, limiting one.

The question that will serve that need is:

Given that it is not true that what people think of you is more important than what you think, what do you think is true and liberating instead?

She ponders this for a while. You listen to her silence. She smiles. She speaks.

What is true and liberating is that true dynamism comes from ease.

Wow, you think. Nice. Glad she didn't hear the one I thought of. So we're there?

No. Just another lantern.

You think about this finding: we reach our desired outcome by embedding the true liberating assumption. Just knowing it is not enough. The challenge is to embed it. That will free her mind to accomplish her current session outcome.

And this is for me the other grateful-to-have-lived-to-see-it bit of knowledge: the mind will embed a true liberating assumption if it can *play* with it. It does that through a question that connects the true assumption and the desired outcome in a *hypothetical* construct.

'If you knew', is hypothetical. So the question has to start that way. And 'how would you' is hypothetical. So the question has to end that way. And in the middle has to be the truth: the true liberating assumption. It is not hypothetical.

In that way the mind gets to play with the truth. The mind wants to play, not to obey. So the embedding construct is: 'If you knew [insert true liberating assumption], how would you [insert desired outcome]?'

Now this seems all pretty clinical, but in practice it is symphonic. So you breeze through the considerations:

We are both still committed to her independent thinking.

What she has just done is construct a liberating, true assumption.

Her session outcome is still to become a relaxed person.

Given that, and the findings about embedding true liberating assumptions, what she needs is to embed the true one.

The question that will serve that need is:

If you knew that true dynamism comes from ease, how would you become a relaxed person?

Her whole body changes. There is vitality and featheriness all at once. She is focused and free, adult and child. She shares some of her thoughts. She would do this and this and this. She holds other thoughts unspoken. She giggles. She ponders.

What a brilliant response, you think. And not a single word of mine in that whole question.

She stops.

I am finished.

You think that result is good enough for a lifetime. But you remember that same finding that showed up twice before: if there have been some waves, there can be more. So you return to the considerations:

We are both still committed to her independent thinking.

What she has just done is to start reaching her session outcome by embedding the true liberating assumption.

Her session outcome is still to become a relaxed person.

Given that and the findings about embedding assumptions, what she needs is to embed the true one more deeply and have more ideas.

The question that will serve that need is:

If you knew that true dynamism comes from ease, how else would you become a relaxed person?

('Else' again.)

More emerges.

And so you do the considerations again. And ask the very same thing again.

And again. And again. Until she has no more thoughts from that question.

You suddenly see why that kind of question is called an incisive question. It did, indeed, incise the untrue limiting assumption by replacing it with this true liberating one and connecting it to her session outcome. What a gigantic job this petite question does.

Is this all?

Almost.

You remember that an incisive question can keep on working after the session and in doing so it further embeds the liberating assumption, affecting more than just this one outcome. Untrue limiting assumptions are usually 'bedrock' like this one was: defining of the self or the world. So holding on to the question is one way for the self to keep growing.

The considerations don't help with this moment. Nature, it seemed, formed the way to the question but not to its preservation! But you do the obvious and propose that she write that last question down in order not to forget it. You tell her that an incisive question is elusive, probably because it so definitively defies and uproots a lifetime untrue assumption. Habits resist demise.

She writes it down. You have to 'correct' it twice, back to her original words, because she has already forgotten a word here and there. Proving the point.

Now is it over?

Nearly.

You know that, as with thinking pairs, good things happen beyond the session if you can appreciate each other as people – not as thinker and partner, just as people – citing a quality you respect in the other.

You do that. It is good.

Now it is over.

How elegant was that?

41. Permutations

You may already suspect that not every thinking session goes exactly like that.

What if, for example, the thinker and criteria disagree?

What would the considerations have said if your thinker had assessed that the untrue limiting assumption ('what people think of me matters more than what I think') was true, or at least possibly true? Given that the assumption in that context is neither factually nor logically provable, how can you get around that impasse? You can use the considerations frame:

Yes, you are both committed to the thinker's independent thinking.

What they have just done is to assess the untrue assumption as true.

Their desired session outcome has not changed.

In light of that and of the findings about this impasse, the thinker needs now to find a liberating alternative that will bypass the untrue assumption they assess is true.

A question that will fill that need is:

You want to become a relaxed person.

You think the assumption is true that what people think of you is more important than what you think.

What could you credibly assume instead in order to become a relaxed person?

I love how the considerations produce a precisely suited question every time. That question I call the 'invitation question' because it invites, rather than imposes, a credible alternative to their untrue assumption. This is a delicate moment because the thinker is holding on to their key assumption as true. And if we can avoid confrontation here, it will assist the thinker to get to their outcome without destroying the thinking environment suddenly.

And what if the thinker proposes different outcomes from the one this thinker chose?

That often happens. A thinker may want, for example, to understand why they do or feel something. Or they may want to focus directly on assumptions in various ways, wanting to start assuming something or to stop assuming something, let's say. Or maybe they want to figure out whether an assumption is true, or just to identify all of the assumptions they are making about something.

All of those kinds of assumption-related outcomes will navigate just a little differently from the one we just experienced. Their navigation would be close, but not exactly the same. The considerations will lead you through the differences.

Or, much more simply, the thinker may want to think about a new topic, something different from the one they explored in the waves before.

Or they may want to get information from somewhere.

Or they may want to get your thinking about what they have been saying.

It isn't practical for us to experience each of those session permutations here. But you can successfully navigate any thinking session if you understand the findings and let the considerations guide you to the next question.

A reminder about the thinker's request for your thinking: this request is not carte blanche for you to share everything you think about what they said, not even through questions. It is a time for you only to address what they really want to know from you. And that may entail your asking them to tell you exactly what their question for you is. You then can answer that question, as briefly as possible, returning to their thinking as a priority.

The main thing is: a thinking session is for one person to go as far as they possibly can in their own thinking about a topic of their choice. At the moment I know of nowhere else on earth we can do this. One day it may be part of everyone's week, and no one will be confused about how to keep it free of 'think for' tendencies in the listener. There just won't be any. There wouldn't dream of being.

For now, though, we can be careful. We can remember that at

any second what the two of us are doing can disappear in the under-
tow of convention and comfortable common practice. And we can
take heart that the human mind will happily return to its full and
real self at the slightest opportunity. In the presence of uncontam-
inated, generative attention, inside the promise of no interruption,
in the hands of the mind's own road of considerations to its own
innate breakthrough questions, it will thunder and hum majestic-
ally. We can make that happen together any time we want to.

I would like to be understated about this, about thinking sessions and how much they accomplish, how adroit they are, how
economical, how changing of a life. I would like just to nod rather
than jump up and down about how different this kind of time with
a person is from any other, how very, very different. I would like to
murmur about how the promise of no interruption changes funda-
mentally how we listen, how we help, how we build the brain and
beauty of another person. But I cannot.

I have the same trouble with Roger Federer. There are no mid-
way things to say about grace that glorious.

42. Just in Case

As the Thinker

You may feel compelled to hand over your thinking to the partner who might not have talked for ages because you have done so much good thinking with their attention and no input at all. You may feel sorry for them. Don't. They will soon realize that the giant resource they are offering you – their generative, uninterrupted attention – probably outstrips any words they could have uttered.

You may think you missed out on some first-class ideas or directions or insights or 'teaching' from them because they did not speak. If so, and if you want those things, just ask. Believe me, they will be only too thrilled to get to speak again.

But the very second their ideas become even a bit enervating, thank them and resume your thinking. When others' thinking enhances you as a thinker, it warrants proceeding. When it erodes you as a thinker, it needs to stop.

What is at stake here is your own mind. The resuscitation of its power, of its galaxies of light and life. Your partner's input is always available to you, but the conditions for your mind to reach and pivot and glissade for itself to territory new, challenging, uniquely yours, are vital and need protecting, even from your own pull to submit to another's view before you have developed your own.

My colleague Trisha Lord says it well: 'Thinking for ourselves takes courage, the courage to reclaim our independence as thinkers. And that courage takes discipline and practice. If we dilute that practice before we have really learned to trust it, we may hijack our independent minds forever.'

You *can* think for yourself all the way to something sound and solid and pragmatic and perfectly whimsical and road-changing and right. You *can*. Your job is to know that. As a thinker your job is to enter the thinking time and not for a second doubt your capacity to think brilliantly, *for yourself.*

You are the only person who can do that.

As the Thinking Partner

You may at first, and sometimes along the way, want more than you have ever wanted anything in your entire life to abandon the promise, to utter just something, anything, in the middle of the thinker's flow. Just to feel alive in the old way. Just to remember what it means to display your proficiency. Don't worry. It happens to all of us. It is only a throwback to that common but limited definition of brilliance: thinking for others. It is easily done.

It comes from assuming you haven't contributed enough because you haven't said enough. You have, exactly because you haven't.

Also, when you do have to ask one of the innate breakthrough questions, you may think they are a consistent string of sequential questions, one leading inexorably to the other, and should all be spoken. They aren't. And you shouldn't. There is no set sequence. One can often be followed by an 'earlier' one or one that 'usually comes later'. The thinker's mind will do such speedy work when it can, that it can easily land 'ahead' of you. And often you can't follow it because it is taking place in the 90 per cent of their thinking that you can't hear. But you don't have to worry about all of that. Through the considerations you will know what to ask next. And it may surprise you how 'out of sequence' it seems. The human mind under these conditions unfolds unpredictably, but coherently.

Combatting the importunate urge to speak without invitation takes only remembering that when the thinker is on an independent roll, it is *because* of your quiet. It is because you are there being truly brilliant, brilliant as the force that ignites *their* mind. You are there understanding the nature and rarity and importance of independent thinking. You are there so masterfully you can stay leagues ahead of the old part of you that wants to talk when talking would silence and reduce the thinker.

It takes only remembering that when the thinker pauses, when they seem to need you to speak but suddenly they take off again, you can rejoice in having not spoken, because they are back into fresh waters, and the waves are fantastic. This is an act of trust in the intelligence before you.

That is your job. To talk as little as possible. To launch as quietly and powerfully as possible. To keep them going *for themselves*.

Never before has so little achieved so much.

There is a law of physics in there somewhere.

And be assured. This is not a solipsistic indulgence in I'm-the-only-real-person-on-the-planet, everyone-else-is-an-abstraction, all-authorities-are-bad kind of thinking. This is a best shot at thinking afresh for one's self in order more intelligently to think with others.

43. Forgiveness: Lotti's Thinking Session

Sometimes the privilege of being a thinking partner is almost too much. Sometimes the thinker goes to places that open not only their own minds, but the minds of anyone listening. To build psychological safety so unalloyed that the thinker can reach the wellspring of truth in their hearts and of wisdom in their experience is so quiveringly consequential as to feel undeserved. Lotti's session with Katie was such a time. They, and the other person on the course who was observing, have given me permission to share this story with you. Now you will be the privileged one.

Lotti was the thinker. Katie was the thinking partner.

'What do you want to think about today?' Katie asked.

Lotti was quiet for several minutes. She squirmed a bit in her chair.

Katie listened.

Eventually Lotti said, 'I know what I *need* to think about. This issue holds me back in my business, my life; it affects everything.'

She paused. They both were quiet.

'I have swept it aside – several times,' she said, 'and maybe I should this time, too.' She paused again. She looked around the room.

'It feels dangerous. I feel I have no right to think about it.'

She was quiet. Katie was quiet.

Then Lotti said, 'I am aware that I am the only German in this group, and I know that Miriam is a Jew. I also know that she is the daughter of Holocaust survivors.'

A few minutes passed. Lotti's silent thought permeated the room.

Eventually she spoke again.

'I feel it is impossible to find the right words. But for my whole life I have needed to try to think about this topic, to talk about it, without being judged. I think it could be possible here. But I am not sure.'

She looked around the group. Everyone was attentive, inter-ested. Their faces were open, encouraging. No one spoke.

'I am forty years old now,' Lotti said. 'When I was a child, I learned that the Germans committed the most awful crime in his-tory and that all Germans are guilty as a nation. We inherited this guilt and were taught that there is no way to remove it without forgetting what happened.

'Every child was taught that. And so were my parents when they were young. The Germans, alive then, and born later, and still to be born. We all are guilty. We were confronted with this in every subject we were taught.'

She stopped. She breathed. She looked at Katie. Katie kept her eyes on Lotti's eyes: with interest, respect, no judgement, no rush, no questions.

'What they said was that at all cost we must never forget, so that it can never, ever happen again. Of course, that is right.

'But they said that the way to keep the memory alive is to accept the guilt.

'And every attempt to talk about it was seen as negating the scope of the atrocities.

'I went to the concentration camp in Dachau with my parents and later to Auschwitz on my own to confront myself with our history.'

Lotti was suddenly quiet. She looked down. And then at Katie.

'That's all for the moment,' she said.

Katie asked gently and slowly, 'What more do you think, or feel, or want to say?'

'In front of the house where we live now,' Lotti said, 'there is a "Stolperstein", the brass memorial plaque commemorating two people who lived in our house before they were deported to Ausch-witz. My son is four years old. Together we polish the Stolperstein, we put flowers and candles there to commemorate the date of their death. We want to keep this memory alive, those two people who used the same front door as we do today.

'But I struggle to know how to explain to my son what

happened. I want him to understand, and to stay alert, but without the guilt.'

She nodded.

'That's all.'

Katie waited and then asked again, 'And what more do you think, or feel, or want to say?'

'Nothing,' Lotti said, 'that's really all for the moment.'

Katie and Lotti looked warmly at each other. Slowly Katie said, 'We still have time. What more, if anything, would you like to accomplish with our session?'

Lotti thought for a while.

'I would like to find a way towards healing,' Lotti said.

She stopped.

'I am not even allowed to have that goal,' she said.

She was quiet for a while.

'Yes,' she said, 'that *is* what I want next to accomplish in this session. I want to find a way towards healing.'

Gently Katie asked Lotti, 'What might you be assuming that is stopping you from finding a way towards healing?'

'I am assuming,' Lotti said, 'that this can't be healed. The Holocaust has created an eternal guilt. I am assuming that to heal is to risk its happening again.'

Katie then asked slowly and gracefully, 'And what else might you be assuming that is stopping you from finding a way towards healing?'

'I assume that I deserve to feel guilty.'

Lotti stopped. She looked at Katie. Her warmth, their quiet, were symbiotic forces.

Lotti cried a bit.

'That is the main assumption,' Lotti said.

'And do you think it is true,' Katie asked gently, 'that you deserve to feel guilty?'

'Yes, I do,' Lotti said.

She was silent. So was Katie.

'A few weeks ago,' Lotti said, 'I got to read letters between my grandparents. I was terrified I would discover that they had been

Nazis. I read and read. And soon I cried. They had not been Nazis. But they had not been heroes, either.

'My friend Stefan also found the letters of his grandmother. "You are lucky," he said to me. "I discovered that my beloved grandma was a committed Nazi. That was the worst day of my life." '

Lotti paused, breathed, looked at Katie.

'I believe that my ancestors are in me,' Lotti said. 'Without them, I would not exist. To be complete as a person I must integrate inside me my ancestors and their heritage.

'And what do I transmit to *my* children if I don't find a way of healing from our history?

'When I have a conflict with my son, I tell him that I disapprove of his action, but I love *him*. And why should that not apply even to the most monstrous criminals? I condemn their actions with my whole being, but who am I to judge the inherent person?'

Lotti was quiet again. Then she said softly, 'No, maybe actually it is not true that I deserve to feel guilty.'

She looked out towards the river.

Then she looked back at Katie.

Katie said gently, 'So, as it is not true that you deserve to feel guilty, what do you think is true and liberating instead?'

Lotti thought for a long time. 'I am thinking about forgiveness,' she said. 'I was taught that to forgive is dangerous because to forgive is to forget. But is it true that to forgive is to forget?'

She thought in silence. After nearly a minute she spoke.

'No,' she said slowly, 'to forgive is to love. Love helps us remember, maybe even more accurately, and then to live differently. If we don't forgive, what is the future?'

She thought more. No one moved.

Lotti said, 'Could you please ask me again, Katie?'

'Of course,' she said. 'If it is not true that you deserve to feel guilty, what do you think is true and liberating instead?'

Lotti thought for a while.

'My ancestors,' she said, 'deserve to be forgiven.' She cried.

Then she nodded, 'That's all.'

Katie waited and then spoke softly. 'And if you knew that your ancestors deserved to be forgiven, how would you find a way towards healing?'

Lotti again was quiet. Eventually she spoke.

'Forgiveness *is* a way towards healing,' she said. 'It integrates a dark side of myself. It brings relief and connection to my grandparents' generation. It empties a gap filled with silent sadness, shame and trauma.'

She paused.

'Could forgiving,' Lotti wondered out loud, 'be the condition for real peace?'

She thought for a while.

'That's all,' she said.

Because people often can generate more, Katie asked again.

'If you knew that your ancestors deserved to be forgiven, how else would you find a way towards healing?'

'I would be more loving and powerful in my work,' Lotti said. She sighed. Her shoulders eased.

Then the time was up.

She smiled. Katie smiled, too.

Lotti wrote down the last question, the 'incisive question', and a few thoughts. She and Katie appreciated each other. The session ended.

Each person on the course then had a turn to say what they had learned.

When it was Miriam's turn, she said, 'Thank you, Lotti.' She cried. She spoke.

'Today I have seen that the Germans were victims, too. It is the Jews who are the victims in the eyes of the world. The Germans are not.

'And yet, barbarity dehumanizes and victimizes *everyone*. To understand this requires the most of each of us. Guilt is not the way. Only forgiveness protects the future.

'Thank you for your courage.'

Lotti thanked her.

This story of personal change and societal restructuring brings us to Einstein. I am sure you know what he said about the desired future: 'We will never get *there* with the thinking that got us *here*.' He was right, of course.

We will get to a new and better world with new and better thinking, brave thinking that dismantles denial, thinking that is the simplicity on the far side of complexity.

Lotti's story reminds me that we can decide today to promise not to interrupt each other and from there to grow a world of fully independent thinking. It will be a formidable job because the world of independent thinking turns lots of our lore and learning inside out, and because that executive was right: it is a step-by-step journey towards humility.

How then do we do it? How do we get formidably good at it? Do we read about it, think about it, talk with others about it, learn more about it? Yes. And we practise – for sixty hours, or 10,000. We require it for the listening professions. We introduce it into teaching and mediation and advising of all kinds.

But maybe, also, we need to do a very different kind of thing. Maybe we need to face regularly into the unknowable, absorbing it, witnessing the conception inside it, being indiscernible in the presence of it.

Every summer I go by myself to New Mexico for a few days. I stay in the enchantment that is Santa Fe. I grew up in New Mexico, so this is an evocation of personal serenity. And it is an encounter with the *unknowable* that echoes through blisteringly incomprehensible timescales before the beginning of life, in which the heart of what matters emerged out of the unassailable reality that nothing mattered. I return to experience that.

Mostly, therefore, my time in New Mexico is a tryst with the sky. I look up. At night as stars emerge, clean against their black canvas, inspired by the philosopher André Comte-Sponville, I work to *stop seeing the stars*. I work to see the black, impenetrable hugeness of the world between the stars. I work to be catapulted into what is most wondrous of all: the making of things from the apparent nothing around them.

I think that in our moments as a thinking partner, in front of us, as we listen, is the night sky. I think that when we create for people the world of fully independent thinking, we are focusing on the space between the stars.

We take in, but are not distracted by, what the thinker has said, or by what we already know. We are drawn instead by what they have not yet even *thought*, by what is in fact unknowable for both of us in that moment.

We have the capacity to be present in that way so that new ideas form, long-awaited insights crystallize, love prevails.

The potential for new thought there is immense.

Our growing the world of independent thinking can, I believe, produce new, breathtaking human systems to fuel our dreams.

We can do this.

We are certainly smart enough.

And maybe, just maybe, we have enough courage.

44. Coaching

The promise of no interruption also changes the way we coach. Coaching, in my view, is one of the best things to have happened to our world. I remember walking across the Sandy Spring Friends School Maryland campus with the Head of the English Department when I was twenty-three. We were talking about how the world could change for the better if everyone had someone who would listen to them and help them think things through. This person would be different from a psychologist or therapist or counsellor or adviser. Wouldn't it be wonderful, we mused, if there were a listening profession that filled that gap?

Fifty years later, here we are.

Coaches, psychologically aware, skilled in all kinds of listening modalities, helping methodologies, thinking frameworks and conceptual models, at ease with emotions, clearly contracted, grounded in the relevant codes of ethics and driven almost always by an authentic, congruent desire to help people move dependably forward, make a difference in people's lives and in the lives of teams and organizations. Coaching is not just a life-changing development; it is a world-improving phenomenon.

I have also loved seeing the profession's increasing interest in independent thinking as the base for client progress. There are now coaches around the world who recognize the so-subtle-as-to-be-nearly-surreptitious nature of contracting for independent thinking as the primary power of the coaching session. Some of these coaches are making the promise of no interruption and the components of a thinking environment, even the practice of full thinking sessions, into the 'core methodology' of their coaching. I would like to talk about that practice in a few minutes. I find it hopeful.

But first, let's say you are a coach. Through your training and experience you will have absorbed all-important learning about how humans tick, and equally effective processes to help them understand and resolve their issues, to reach their goals, to realize themselves, to be emotionally literate, to live and lead from intelligent empathy, to be successful in the broadest possible context. You will arrive at each session with this valuable 'toolbox'.

More importantly, you will also bring to each session your refined ability to see what the client is not seeing, to find beneath their words and stories common themes and patterns and assumptions.

(Note that I use the word 'client', not 'coachee', a popular appellation for the thinker in a coaching session. I know that coaches who use that term do not mean to reduce the thinker to a diminutive subset of the coach. But effectively it does that, I think. Inequality stealthily infects language. You might well ask what we can do, though, about 'mentor/mentee'. I don't know. But at least in mentoring there is a bit of built-in legitimate differential of experience or authority.)

You will strive to be true to the coach's commitment not to tell people what to do but to formulate questions that you think will take them in their chosen direction, or in one even better.

You will 'challenge' your clients, focus them on the hard questions, the inconsistencies, the self-deception, even the duplicities that burden their journeys.

Your work is stellar. Some say consistently.

And in all of these ways you will be giving value to your clients beyond any fee they could pay you. Your clients are thinking better and better. And the results are striking.

How, then, is it different to work with a client in a thinking environment? Isn't that what coaches are doing every day? A coaching colleague said to me recently, 'The thinking environment and its promise of no interruption is like the "unified field theory of coaching".' What could he possibly have meant? What is it that the singular purpose of fully independent thinking does? What exactly in our coaching does the promise of no interruption change?

Everything.

I don't mean that we lose one single piece or dimension of our other coaching expertise. Everything we know and everything we now bring to our client remains. Riches like that only grow in value.

I do mean that we face in a different direction.

We face towards our client's unthought thoughts.

We face away from our already formulated ones. We face away from our urge to take them to ours. We face away from our 'known', and towards their 'not yet known'.

I do mean that we change what we wonder about.

We wonder how far our client can go in their own thinking before they need ours.

We wonder how much further even than that they can go. We stop wondering when to come in, when to speak, what question will best advance the take we already have on where they need to go.

I do mean that we shift our trust.

We trust the intelligence in front of us.

We trust less the primacy of our own thinking. We trust more the irreplaceable unpredictability of theirs.

I do mean that we recognize that a person is saying only about 10 per cent of what they are thinking, and that any decision we make about what to offer them is missing 90 per cent of their thought.

I do mean that we recognize also that we cannot know for sure that what we are about to say will be of greater value than what they are about to think.

I do mean that we change how we determine a session's value.

We open our eyes to the inestimable gain of the client's own, fresh, finest thinking. And we evaluate the session by noticing how much of that independent thinking it produced.

We tell our clients that they will be paying for our attention. We say that all the rest is a bonus.

I do mean that we recognize what 'challenging the client' really entails. We recognize that when our client thinks their way deeply into their own hardest seeing, into their own downing of denial, into their own unthinkable questions and on to their own cutting edge, freeing themselves of debilitating and heartless untrue assumptions without our pointing out a single one, they meet the fiercest challenges. We see that our 'challenges', while useful and appreciated, pale in comparison to their own.

I do mean that we contract consciously for the perfect proportions of thinking session and coach direction.

We agree from the start that the coaching session will be inside the promise of no interruption. We confirm that as the coach we will not speak without invitation from the client. We agree that the coaching session will start with a formal thinking session, and will take an agreed proportion of the total session time. We agree that in the remaining portion of the session, even though we now will be in dialogue, we will not interrupt the client, and that the client will speak far more than we will. We agree that every additional tool we may propose as coach will be conducted in a thinking environment, guided by all of the ten behaviours and the ways they express the promise.

That changes everything. That gains everything. And loses nothing.

In the same way that I can imagine a time when people live in a thinking environment from birth to death, when everyone's finest independent thinking is the starting point and the main point, when respect is this pervasive, I also can imagine a time when coaching is by definition a place where the independent mind of the client develops as it progresses practical issues.

Some coaches say that the coaching profession is not up for this. They say that a thinking session cannot become the core of a coach's approach, that the promise of no interruption cannot prevail as the fundamental culture of a coaching session. They claim that if coaching is anything, it is the offering by the coach and the challenging by the coach and the in-the-moment inserting by the coach of their highly trained, professional insights and expertise. They say that this is what the client wants to pay for, that no one will pay for uninterrupted attention. They say that people do not value their own thinking, and so they will not pay someone to help them produce it.

People can get aggressive about this. I once was demonstrating this process, and after five minutes of uninterrupted listening, the client shouted with bared teeth and a growl, 'Coach me!' In effect he meant, 'Think for me!' We stopped and talked about coaching as direction rather than fresh independent thinking, and in the end agreed not to go on.

Someone also said once that the thinking session, the whole thinking environment in fact, consists of only two things: attention and assumptions. When I heard that, I was tempted to fume. What an experience-dry, knowledge-dry assessment that was, I thought. For two seconds.

Then I realized that in a certain sense, a wonderful sense, it was true. And who could ask for more? Attention generates breathtaking breakthroughs, and assumptions are the main reason why.

And almost all coaches would agree, I think, that coaching at its best, any listening work at its best, wants in the end to have done one thing above everything: to generate breakthrough thinking. To know as a coach that the thinking session can do exactly that virtually every time, and can, along the way, develop the client's ability to think better and better, is to fulfil the main purpose of coaching. The coach's additional offerings are indeed a priceless bonus. But only a bonus.

So how does this thinking-session-based coaching look? However my client requests. Clients range hugely in how they structure the sessions. One, without planning it per se, uses about 60 per cent of the time for the thinking session, 40 per cent for my thoughts and our dialogue. Another rarely wants my thinking at all; he progresses his issues entirely from my attention, and impressively. Three clients use a full hour for a thinking session, and the second hour to ask me questions, request my take and think about my response. That response takes many forms: sharing of experience or knowledge, offering of insights, challenging incoherence or denial, lobbing back questions about their questions, presenting occasionally a particular other framework or model. But always, always, briefly and with a return to the client as thinker.

And always, always, always without interruption of them.

I am also watching with interest another take on the thinking session as coaching. Some people are offering, especially to clients in organizations, a thinking session separately from a 'classic' coaching session. I can see how this might work. And at the very least, it could be a client's easy transition to thinking-session-based coaching.

Some people also are teaching their clients, particularly the ones who are leaders and executives, how to do thinking sessions themselves so that they and a trusted colleague or associate can become thinking partners regularly. I particularly like this move because it has always been my hope that the thinking session will become a regular, invaluable part of our lives, for free. At most we would have only to pay to learn it. It would then be ours forever.

More permutations of thinking-session expressions of the promise not to interrupt will evolve I am sure. I am looking forward to it all eagerly.

Coaching has come such a long and beautiful distance. I celebrate it. And I look forward to its next stage which, I predict, may look a lot like this.

It deserves to. The world needs it to. And our clients, the second they sense the chance, want it to.

We can make sure that it does.

45. *Leading*

' "I won't interrupt you" changed the way I lead,' Charles told me.

'It also changed the way I develop young leaders. As chief executive I have generally been a good listener. At any rate, people say so. But understanding the promise of no interruption moved me from good listener to generator of independent thinking, almost overnight. And over a period of time it moved the organization from just producer of choice goods to producer of choice minds. And all without fanfare or millions on culture change. Understanding the promise is the simplest, most profound and most cost-effective change I think we have ever undertaken. And I am not a hyperbolist. I try to keep my wishful thinking out of my assessment thinking.'

I asked Charles how he did it.

I did four things (with a lot of subsets). Anyone can do them. You just have to want to do them and get the results more than you want to be right, to dominate, to show off, to keep people afraid of you or to be comfortable. That's the complicated part. The promise itself is simple.

First, I told people *why* I wanted to make this change: we need the best ideas around here and if we *promise* not to interrupt each other, ideas will increase and improve. I explained that not interrupting is more sophisticated than merely shutting up and waiting for someone to finish, that it means giving people attention driven by interest in where they will go next with their thinking, being proportional in our turns, not hogging the show.

Second, we changed our meetings. Amazingly, Andrew Ellson's article on meetings that I read in the *Sunday Times*, confirms almost exactly our experience of meetings. Just as he says, we spend half our working week in meetings, and at least a third of that time is wasted, mostly by interruption that delays us or takes us off track and by people checking their phones more than a third of the time. Also, people daydream part of the time because only a few people do the thinking and talking.

So the promise of no interruption is now the culture of all our meetings. And that takes many forms. For example:

We now give careful thought to the agenda ahead of time, knowing we want it to generate, not interrupt, people's best thinking. So we take each agenda topic. We figure out the question inside the topic which is what we really need to be addressing. Ahead of time people receive the agenda in the form of questions. They get to the meeting already thinking. Questions make you think, instantly. Phrases put you to sleep.

Also, I like the point Christopher Spence made that 'until people have spoken, they haven't arrived'. So we make sure that through rounds everyone gets to speak (and think) about every item. And here I take with me another of his points. This one is really important because it just wouldn't occur to you: doing rounds with no interruptions takes courage. It does. It counters just about everything people have experienced in their whole meeting life, and they say are comfortable with, even if they hate it in private. Somehow it helps to know that rounds are a kind of revolutionary and courageous act of leadership.

Anyway, we open each meeting with a round. We look at the positive reality by doing a 'success round', asking a question like: 'What is going well in your work at the moment?'

Then we do rounds for every agenda item.

We follow each round with open discussion where anyone can speak but never interrupt or tailgate.

Sometimes we divide into thinking pairs or dialogues to consider the question first, always keeping the promise.

And we come back to another round, not to say what we came up with, but rather what our freshest thinking is now. That allows the round to produce new thoughts as well.

We are disciplined about digital devices (the great stupefiers of meetings, I have found), putting them away unless we all need to consult them for something. And we have just about done away with PowerPoint. We could all soon see that the minute the slide goes up, the attention for and from the presenter goes down. And because it is our connection with the presenter and the presenter's with us that keeps people thinking during the presentation, Power-Point is self-defeating.

It also makes lazy presenters of people, allowing them to rely on the slide as a crutch. If we absolutely have to have a graph or illustration to make the point, we use a handout or send a slide to people's pads which they disable after that part of the presentation. This PowerPoint habit was the hardest to kick. But the quality of thinking and engagement has risen noticeably. And nobody cried or died.

At the end of the meeting we have a quick round to say what we thought went well in the meeting (even if it was hard); and then, once a month, we say something we respect about whoever is next to us.

The simplicity and effectiveness of this is ridiculous.

Third, we have a thinking council once a month, at least. One person on the team presents an issue they want help with. They think about it for a few minutes and come up with the question they want the others of us to address. We answer any questions about the question itself. And then everyone takes a two-minute turn to offer their thinking on the question, but only as experience and knowledge, not advice. Everyone else, including the presenter, gives attention. We record it so the presenter can refer to it later. And then we each say a word of respect for the presenter. Everyone likes the council. It benefits everyone. It also keeps developing the team. Anyway, we wouldn't be without it now.

Fourth, we save time. By enacting the promise of no interruption, first one to one and then in meetings, I demonstrate how it saves us time, a finding that is counter-intuitive (or at least counter-cultural) in the extreme. I love how sceptical people were of this time-saving feature at first, and how amazed they then were to see it in action. Then gradually because we knew that the promise would save us time, we just became less frantic. And, interestingly, the promise seems to work better proportionate to how little rush and urgency there is. The promise and ease enlarge each other in that way. That intrigues me.

So we have turned our typically adrenaline-caked, brain-frying office into a really, really alive and generally relaxed (and I have to say respectful, as well as smart) place to work. No one thought that a) we could do it or b) we'd have better results from it. But we did, and we do.

And you know, we have seven corporate values. We spent a lot of money figuring them out and carving them into the wall. They're good. But sometimes people leave because our leaders push the values but don't practise them. What is amazing, though, is that a thinking environment automatically makes us live those values. Respect, inclusion, innovation, individuality, dignity, leadership, courage – all of them.

Who would have thought that this promise could be such a force? We know that knowledge is a force; it creates truth. We know that experience is a force; it creates perspective. But who would have thought that attention is a force? It creates thought.

It is the 'how' for so much.

Charles is out there just doing this. He's not making a big roll-out deal of it. He is using his influence wherever he can to make it happen. Some people on the edges say they are noticing the positive changes in his teams. But he just smiles. He says he knows that the changes the promise is making in how he leads and in how his teams perform are entirely predictable. It's just what knowing you won't be interrupted does. It's not complicated.

I think about Charles and his teams often. I want every leader to listen as Charles does. I want leaders to generate good thinking from people. I want them to know, as Cal Newport does (and as I learned from William Park's article in BBC Global News, 15 July

2019), that the next great revolution in the office will recognize that 'the value someone can bring to a company will be . . . not . . . their skill, but . . . their ability to focus'. I want leaders to know that this revolution needs the promise of no interruption from the first minute of the day to the last. It needs the keeping of it, too. And the remembering that just shutting up is entirely not the point. Being interested in the thinking that is evolving is. I love that Charles gets that.

'Does the thinking environment work its wonders in a virtual meeting as well?' Leaders ask about this hungrily because teams more than ever are meeting online, and this trend will only grow. The answer is yes. Up to a point.

As we saw earlier in reference to the component of place and to virtual-thinking sessions, virtual meetings cannot reproduce the same calibre of generative attention that in-person meetings can. And for reasons research is uncovering by the minute now, online meetings, even in a thinking environment, can be exhausting. (See *National Geographic*, April 2020.)

But people can be thrilled by virtual meetings held in a thinking environment because they are miles better and more productive than their usual meetings. And so increasingly Charles and other leaders are transposing their thinking environment structures from in-person to online. The results so far are significant.

Leadership is the conscious creation of culture. I am heartened that more and more leaders around the world are understanding this, and they are understanding that the promise of no interruption will be – because it has to be – the future culture of leadership. Again, we can't get where we want to go as a conscious, human-and-earth-connected business world with the thinking that got us here. And fresh, 'just right' thinking arises under certain conditions. The promise of no interruption is a key to them all.

Leaders like these are 'intentional' leaders. Through this promise, and its complex simplicity, they build connection and thus a culture of psychological safety, and then of courageous, results-rich, integrated thinking. They walk through the day restoring dignity to each person. They spread levels of commitment that no amount of *rah-rah* could ever achieve. They speak with their listening. They grow the intelligence of people with their promise to wonder how far people can go with their thinking and what they will think next. They save time. They make better decisions. They produce an authentic, effective, changed and better organization. All because of one promise, taken seriously, practised concertedly, modelled with ease.

And not just in business.

In schools, too.

In many parts of the world now the people who hold in their hands the lives of children and their futures are gradually creating thinking environments as their primary way of leading. Principals, teachers and school-board members are increasingly turning their schools into places where the independent thinking of each colleague is the aim. Leaders of preschool through high school are experiencing the systemic promise of no interruption and the thinking environment it creates.

Perhaps you think the accomplishment here is trivial because schools, surely, should already be a thinking environment. They should. But they aren't. Not usually. How could it be otherwise? Wherever professionals gather, even educators, a think-for-others culture will tag along. All of us, in every profession, are told that we add value mostly by offering our thinking. No one said much about adding value by offering our attention. No one said that our primary job was to ignite independent minds all around us. Fill them, yes. Direct them, yes. Focus them, yes. Unleash them, not so much.

But in South Africa, school principals are telling a different story. You may already have heard of 'Partners For Possibility'. It is the brainchild of Louise van Rhyn. I am following its progress through one of its inspiring leaders, Robyn Whittaker. Through this structure school principals pair with business leaders to become partners in thinking about and solving the challenges in education in South Africa. Groups of partners then meet regularly to think together about each school's issues, and to progress them together.

The partners also go through a dynamic leadership development programme, a key piece of which is the thinking environment. The principals then apply their learning to their leading of faculty and they in turn to the teaching of children.

I love that this is happening in the world. It has always seemed to me that the best way to support the education of children is to support the development of people who deliver it. And according to these pioneers, the expertise of creating thinking environments for meetings and dialogue in their faculties and eventually as classroom culture is transformative.

I have been especially moved by the leadership of Charlotte Mpho Ndwambi, principal of Makhoarane Primary School, who is putting all of the components of a thinking environment into practice throughout her school. I would love to hear ten years from now from the children who will be the beneficiaries of her courageous stewardship.

And on the other side of the world, building the leadership prowess of youth in their early twenties, Audrie Semeona Frias, programme officer at the Council of Asian Liberals and Democrats, is, through the work of Trisha Lord, engaging young leaders in Cambodia, the Philippines, Indonesia, Hong Kong, Malaysia, Thailand, Singapore and Taiwan in the thinking environment as vital leadership expertise. Naresh Buddalongaiwan of Singapore said of this learning:

> I can clearly recall the value-added nature of the Thinking Environment and how it improved the quality of communication between my group members and me. Actively using it as the guiding force in our open discussions, each of us felt heard, represented and appreciated. As such, we were able to think more critically about situations and challenges that we were faced with. It was an obvious difference from the regular group discussions that I have had prior to this event.

Leadership like this is doing humanity a particular favour. When we create thinking environments as the culture of our organizations (and lives), we are doing a fascinating thing that Nassim Taleb describes in *Antifragile*. (If you haven't read that book, sit down right now and read it. You might need to take a short leave of absence from your job because this book is both difficult to read and difficult to put down. And entirely worth it.)

But right now consider his key point: when serious upheaval, massive stress and unwanted change come along, it is not so great to be 'fragile to them' (as Taleb would say). It is better to be resilient to them. But it is best to be 'antifragile' to them. That is, it is best actually to *benefit* from them. That is not to say that we should create near-catastrophes or times of debilitating stress in order to benefit from them. But when they happen, we want to find a way to benefit from them, not just recover from them.

The relevant point here is that when our lives are largely in a thinking environment, we become antifragile. We have the resources and the developed mental capacity to think our way ingeniously through the crisis together, and to arrive better than we were before. Leaders who can rally people around that idea will move their organizations more successfully from crisis to benefit. I find that very exciting.

You can lead like this. You can take that idea and every other idea in this book and get started. You first can get good at it by doing it yourself here and there. Leaders have to be a reference point for people first, not a mouthpiece. And then you can start slowly. Turn just one agenda item into a question, for example, and propose an uninterrupted round. See how it goes. Usually it is superb. People will want more.

Then you're set. They will trust you. They will do it all. Gratefully.

'Leadership for a Thinking Environment' has been my company's 'strapline' for decades. But I feel I am just beginning to understand what it means.

46. Media

The changes the promise makes in broadcast media are seam-ripping. But I'll keep this short. As they would.

Please could interviewers and panellists stop interrupting their guests and each other? I know you are trying to hold people accountable, and I appreciate that. But you are holding their best thinking, and ours, and probably your own, to ransom.

Thank you.

Oh, and could you find out how Michael Barbaro, Judy Woodruff and Clare Balding achieve no interruption so brilliantly? And then do it yourselves?

Thanks.

PS Your children are watching.

47. *From Here*

Imagine if we were to see the usurping of the human mind all around us and decide to re-seize it. Imagine if we were to generate fresh independent thinking wherever we go, to promise not to interrupt each other, to listen all the way through to something new. Imagine if we were to think for ourselves in the face of the mind-stripping conformity of economics; to give a little there-there pat to our hand-top platforms and rouse them only a few times a day; to resist the pull of persuasion; and to reconnect with each other, no longer polarized.

Imagine if we were to ask often:

What do you think?
And what more?

And to mean:

I want to know what you think.
I won't interrupt you.
I promise.

And if people were to reciprocate? What might change for us? And our world?

How might life look on the other side of those momentous, but simple, decisions?

We could decide to see. It is true we will find no certainty here because real life loves to wonder; real life builds without blueprint, without bricks, without code. Real life *occurs*.

But inside that lush uncertainty we can see that in here, in our *self*, in our thinking core, is the assurance we seek. We can count on our *selves*. We can count on our very own minds and hearts to burst with exuberance and authenticity and efficacy every time. Every time we decide to think for ourselves. Every time we create the conditions. Every time we respect each other this much.

So, let's go. Let's run into the arms of each other's attention and look into the eyes of each other's intelligence.

Understanding the promise of no interruption is almost a sacred undertaking. It requires commitment to Nature.

It is more than a shift in philosophy because it is an earthquake in practice.

It is more demanding than an initiative because it cannot be shelved.

It brings peace but no rest because it demands our best.

Once seen, it cannot be unseen.

And that is good. We cannot sanction the old any longer. We cannot bear to return to interruption and its rapiers. The only thing for us now is the gradual but tipping-point-destined unravelling of the behaviour that led us, also gradually, to this will-we-make-it moment in our species' sojourn.

But seeing, experiencing, understanding the promise of no interruption is to breathe life into the promise of a future Nature made to us at our conception. Returning to her, returning to the built-in power of no interruption of each other's thinking, we move, one moment, then another, inexorably to that world we expected. This kind of moving builds. And builds.

The promise of no interruption changes everything.

Last Word

I have loved this time with you.

I've savoured the splashing of our feet and the light on the water. Our wonderings and wanderings and ponderings and peerings and peace have moved me. Being with you has helped me see afresh what the promise can do.

We have seen that we need no torch if our path is forged each moment by our own bearings. If no one is trampling before we wake, we need only step and step again, and we are there. The promise of no interruption leads and follows and fine-tunes and finishes and lifts the baton again and we can catch our thoughts and toss them and let them settle softly and fiercely and perfectly and chaotically and with sculpted abandon until we sit for tea and giggle and suddenly rise.

Thinking for ourselves is the real music of the spheres. It is the desire and the reason, the thirst and the dew. It plays and bows and sings us to sleep and to wake and to love, and to ideas that have so long languished, aching to form, reaching to the heaven that is attention, the promise, and the silent, silky sureness of the human mind freed and formidable and fine.

Yours and mine.

Thank you.

Acknowledgements

Acknowledgements are funny things. They pluck out of a sky of encouragement a few stars and leave unnamed the rest of the firmament. So please know that only if you were to lie under the Montana night sky would you see as many lights as made this book possible. I am grateful to every one.

The named ones here contributed directly to the book over these three years.

Thank you . . .

Sheila Crowley – Literary Agent, Curtis Brown – for your indefatigable belief in these ideas and in me, for your grace in navigating both the heart and the product, and for the joy you bestow everywhere.

Venetia Butterfield – Publishing Director, Penguin Life, Penguin Random House, editor – for you as radiant seer: of the importance of thinking environments in our beleaguered world, of my readiness to write this book and of beauty at the centre of everything.

Christopher Spence – beloved husband, thinker, listener, editor – for your finely calibrated steps between enlightening and trusting, for helping me to 'go deep' and for your love of words and of the writer in me.

Bill Godwin – scientist, philosopher, model of independent thinking – for teaching me the importance (and joy) of being wrong in order to get closer to being right.

Marion Miketta – teacher, leader, embodiment of grace and courage – for your Lotti.

Maryse Barak – teacher, thinking partner, changer of lives, articulator of essence – for seeing the 'territory of possibility'.

Megan Dawe – beauty creator and impressive perceiver of human beings – for definitive 'yeses' when they mattered most.

Merl Glasscock – beloved big sister, intrepid voice for justice and dignity – for being my lionheart.

Ruth McCarthy – teacher, collaborator, innovator, co-thinker – for believing in this book, for refining its title, for being a Reader, for Vanilla Pod days and all days.

Stephanie Archer – Business Director, Time To Think – for being a Reader, and for living the core of this book and championing the core of me.

Trisha Lord – teacher, discerner, pioneer, thinking partner – for emboldening and freeing my life, including my writing, every Sunday afternoon, for being a Reader and for developing leaders of the future.

Vanessa Helps – thirty-year-dear friend and muse – for 'Stockbridge' and for sitting at the heart of every book about this I have written.

'Wonderfuls' – faculty, collegiates, graduates, students – for our discoveries, and for treasuring the unexplored edge.

Essential Reading

You probably shouldn't leave home before you read these books at least once:

Adams, Scott, *Win Bigly: Persuasion in a World Where Facts Don't Matter*, New York, NY, USA: Portfolio Penguin, 2017

Appiah, Kwame Anthony, *The Lies That Bind: Re-thinking Identity – Creed, Country, Colour, Class, Culture*, London, UK: Profile Books, 2018

Crawford, Matthew B., *The World Beyond Your Head: On Becoming an Individual in an Age of Distraction*, New York, NY, USA: Farrar, Straus and Giroux, 2015

Eisenstein, Charles, *Climate: A New Story*, Berkeley, CA, USA: North Atlantic Books, 2018

Maturana Romesin, Humberto, and Verden-Zöller, Gerda, *The Origin of Humanness in the Biology of Love*, Exeter, UK: Imprint Academic, 2008

Taleb, Nassim Nicholas, *Antifragile*, London, UK: Allen Lane, Penguin Books, 2012

Williams, James, *Stand Out of Our Light: Freedom and Resistance in the Attention Economy*, Cambridge, UK: Cambridge University Press, 2018

Index